Discovery of
the North

Discovery of the North

THE EXPLORATION OF CANADA'S ARCTIC

Daniel Francis

Hurtig Publishers
Edmonton

Hurtig Publishers Ltd.
10560 – 105 Street
Edmonton, Alberta
Canada   T5H 2W7

Canadian Cataloguing in Publication Data

Francis, Daniel.
  Discovery of the North

Includes index.
Bibliography: p. 213
ISBN 0-88830-280-0 (bound).

1. Canada, Northern — Discovery and exploration.
2. Arctic Regions — Discovery and exploration.
I. Title.
FC3961.F72 1985   971.9'901   C85-091072-2
F1090.5.F72 1985

Hurtig Publishers acknowledges the financial support of the Government of Canada through the Canadian Studies Directorate of the Department of the Secretary of State of Canada.

Design by Bob Young/BOOKENDS DESIGNWORKS

Maps prepared by Luc Gauvin, Departement de Cartographie, CEGEP de Limoilou, Quebec.

Printed and bound in Canada by D.W. Friesen & Sons Ltd.

Contents

Illustrations

Photographs *following pages* 32 *and* 208

Maps

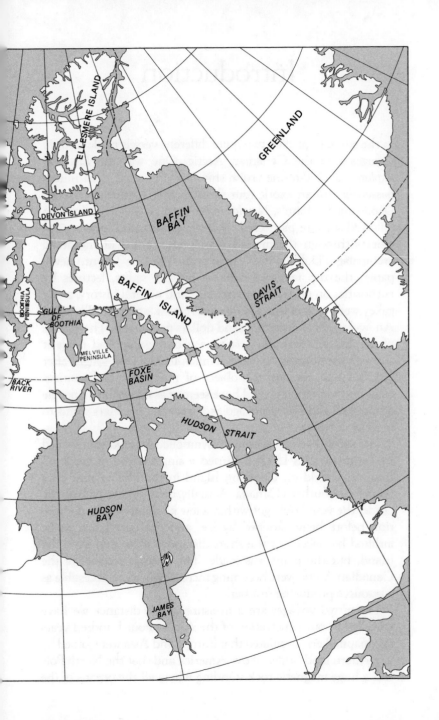

Introduction

In the summer of 1984 two quite different vessels made historic voyages into the Canadian Arctic. One was the *Lindblad Explorer*, a 2200-tonne cruise ship carrying more than ninety passengers on an exotic tour through the Northwest Passage. Departing St. John's, Newfoundland, in August, the *Explorer* followed a route pioneered by several nineteenth-century explorers through the myriad islands and straits of the arctic archipelago. Dubbed the "caviar cruise" by one Toronto newspaper, the trip featured visits to historic sights, lectures by authorities on northern archaeology and natural history, and a galley well stocked with champagne, caviar, and pâté. The cost? An average of twenty thousand dollars per person. The voyage of the *Explorer* was the first time a cruise ship had made it through the passage. At last this much-feared, long-sought-after channel had become the object of post-cards and tourists' cameras. Such a trip would have seemed as incredible to people a hundred and fifty years ago as a weekend on Mars seems to most of us today.

The second voyage was more symbolic. A cargo ship owned by Panarctic Oils Limited carried a single barrel of crude oil from an oilfield on Cameron Island in the High Arctic to a refinery in southern Canada. Actually, on its way to pick up the crude, the vessel only got within a few kilometres of its destination before being stopped by ice, and the barrel had to be airlifted by helicopter the short distance to the ship from the island, but the point was made. The deepest recesses of the Canadian Arctic were becoming increasingly more accessible as a resource-producing frontier.

These two voyages are a measure of the distance we have travelled in our penetration of the Arctic. Four hundred years ago mapmakers speculated that Europe and Asia were joined by a northern land bridge above America and that the North Pole was a huge magnetic rock standing where all the oceans of the world converged. Not much more than a hundred years ago some scientists believed that the top of the world was covered in a temperate, ice-free Polar Sea. Today we know more about the true nature of the arctic world, but still we seek to understand and exploit it.

This book tells the story of exploration in the Arctic from the voyages of Martin Frobisher in the 1570s to the final assertion of Canadian sovereignty in the area in the 1920s. Before Frobisher, mariners visited the archipelago but the visits were sporadic and poorly documented. Frobisher marks the beginning of a sustained assault on the secrets of the North. By the 1920s the age of "heroic exploration" was over. The North was becoming a scientific and resource frontier; the land masses and navigable sea routes had for the most part been recognized and surveyed.

In the story about the growth of knowledge of the Canadian arctic archipelago, little contribution was made by Robert Peary and his rivals in the race for the North Pole. Consequently, these well-known expeditions have not been included here. Similarly, the activities of the Russians in Alaska, and their relations with the Americans, belong to a different story and are not discussed. In other words, *Discovery of the North* is an account of the *Canadian* North and how that territory came to be mapped and legally defined.

The history of exploration is no more than a chapter in the history of the North. It touches only obliquely on the lives of the native people who inhabit the area and whose presence long predates the arrival of the first discoverers. The success of many expeditions depended on the help of local people; indeed, one of the themes of arctic exploration is the gradual adoption of native techniques by European travellers. However, the history of exploration is largely the history of European and American activity in the North. During the same period the Indians and Inuit went about their daily lives indifferent to the motives and mishaps of the intruders from far away.

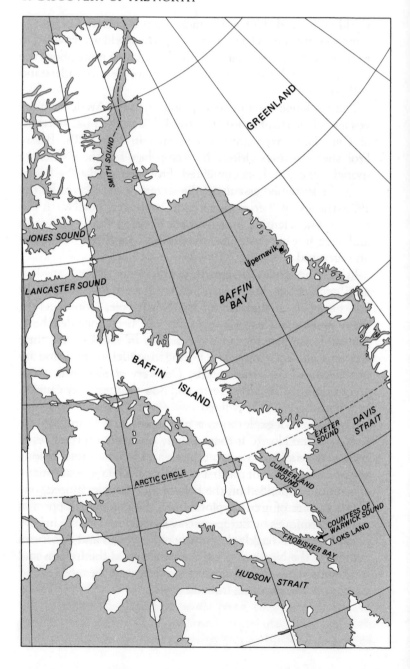

1

The First
Voyages

On August 19, 1576, Martin Frobisher left his sailing ship *Gabriel* anchored in the lee of a tiny, offshore island, rowed to the beach and climbed to the summit of a rocky hill on what he took to be the coastline of northern Asia. As he gazed across the narrow "strait" which he had been exploring for almost a month, he saw to the south the looming shadow of the American mainland, or so he believed. More importantly, as he looked to the west in the direction he was heading he saw many signs that the course he had set himself would soon bring him to the Western Ocean and the shores of China. For Frobisher believed that he had penetrated the passage to Cathay and that all the riches of the Orient and the East Indies would soon be open to him. "There he saw far the two head lands at the furdest end of the straiets," wrote one of the chroniclers of the voyage, "and no likelyhood of land to the northwards of them and the great open betwene them which by reason of the great tydes of flood which they found comming owt of the same, and for many other reasons they judged to be the West Sea, whereby to pass to Cathay and to the East India."

Unhappily for Frobisher, and the English merchants who had sent him, he was not on the verge of a great discovery. The passage to Cathay, the elusive Northwest Passage across the top of America, would remain an unsolved mystery for another three centuries. Instead of standing on the coast of Asia, Frobisher was in fact standing on the coast of what would later be called Baffin Island in the arctic archipelago north of Labrador. The "strait" he was exploring was the deep bay which now bears his name and up ahead, where he so eagerly sought the way through, was not the Western Ocean, but a dead end.

However, Frobisher was spared the disappointment of discovering his mistake. On their way back to the *Gabriel*, he and his men made initial contact with the local Inuit who had been watching the strangers from a wary distance. Gifts were exchanged and after the ship's master, Christopher Hall, went ashore among them, the Inuit felt secure enough to board the vessel, bringing with them sealskin and bearskin coats which the sailors traded for "belles, looking glasses, and other toyes." Using sign language, Frobisher asked one of the local men to guide his ship the rest of the way through the passage. The man agreed and was taken in the boat by five seamen to get his kayak and prepare for the voyage. At this point amicable relations between Inuit and Europeans broke down in an incident which poisoned all future dealings between Frobisher and the local people. In spite of their commander's cautious order not to approach the main body of the Inuit, the five sailors deposited their passenger on shore and immediately rowed out of sight behind an island, probably to trade further with the natives. Whether the Inuit took them captive, whether there was bloodshed, whether the sailors attempted to cheat or rob their new trading partners, no one knows. The five men were never seen again.

When his men did not return, Frobisher concluded they had

been taken captive and he determined to take his own hostage against their safe return. The Inuit were now leery but after a few days Frobisher was able to attract one of them close to the ship. It was the same man who had agreed to pilot the vessel. Displaying various items of trade as bait, Frobisher lured the man in his kayak closer and closer until finally, leaning over the side to hand him a bell, he grasped the native by the arm and heaved him, still in the kayak, onto the ship's deck. The Inuk was so angry "he bit his tongue in twayne within his mouth," according to one report. But Frobisher's strategy did not work. The other Inuit withdrew and did not come forward to negotiate. After waiting several days for something to happen, Frobisher had no choice but to return to England. An armed rescue attempt would have been useless. The ship's boat was gone, and even if the sailors got ashore the Inuit had shown their ability to melt away into the landscape. Time was passing—it was by now late in August—and the men were "tyred and sik with laboure of their hard voyage." The loss of five men and the boat seriously hampered plans for further exploration anyway. So, keeping the Inuit captive, perhaps as a present for Queen Elizabeth, Frobisher sailed back down his "streyte" and out into the North Atlantic.

Back in England, Frobisher's voyage to the northwest was considered a great success. First of all he seemed to have discovered the passage to Cathay. The existence of such a passage was taken for granted in his day. There were several garbled stories of expeditions that had sailed into it, and most cosmographers and mapmakers incorporated the passage into their visions of the world. In the sixteenth century it was recognized that America was an island; but what might its northern regions look like? Abhorring blank spaces on their maps, early cartographers concocted all sorts of theories.

According to one widely accepted hypothesis, America was overarched by a land bridge connecting northeastern Asia to northwestern Europe via Greenland. The Northwest Passage flowed between the land bridge and America, beginning in the Atlantic somewhere not far north of Labrador and trending west and south before emptying into the Pacific in the vicinity of modern-day Oregon State. This was the opinion of Sir Humphrey Gilbert, whose "Discourse of a Discoverie for a new Passage to Cataia" appeared in 1576, the year of Frobisher's first voyage, a fact which probably explains the explorer's conviction that he was sailing between two great continents.

Other geographers believed that the northern land bridge was not continuous, that Asia and Europe did not join but that instead an area of broken islands and open seas lay above America all the way to the North Pole. Speculation about the polar world has always encouraged the fantasist. One account dating from the fourteenth century imagined a polar sea surrounded by a circle of islands broken by nineteen channels. Through these channels water from the southern seas rushed to converge on a single whirlpool spiralling down into the earth. At the centre of the whirlpool, at the top of the world, stood a gigantic, black, magnetic rock. George Best, who sailed with Frobisher and whose account of the voyages was published in 1578, echoed this early description in his own discussion of the land north of America. According to Best, the polar islands were located in about latitude 70° N and numbered just four. They were separated by "foure greate guttes, indraftes, or channels, running violently, and delivering themselves into a monstrous receptacle, and swallowing sincke, with suche a violent force and currant, that a Shippe being entred never so little within one of these foure indraftes, cannot be holden backe by the force of any great winde, but runneth in headlong by that deepe swallowing sincke, into the bowels of the earth." One of the northern islands was inhabited by pygmies; another had a temperate climate and fertile soil for planting. "Al these indraftes and raging channels, runne directly towards a point under the Pole, where is also said to be a monstrous gret Mountain of wonderful gret height..." It was Best's contention that Frobisher's passage divided America not from Asia but from these polar islands.

Frobisher's voyages are a perfect example of the marriage of commercial and geographic interest that motivated arctic exploration until the nineteenth century. They were part of a series of English ventures which had begun in the previous century with John Cabot's expeditions to Newfoundland in the 1490s. While Cabot's account of the Grand Banks sparked interest in the cod fishery, subsequent voyages continued to seek a way around or through America. To anyone but a fisherman, this new continent was in the road, blocking a clear passage to the East Indies and the precious gems, spices, and cloth these exotic lands produced. The Portuguese and Spanish were aggressive competitors for eastern trade and in the sixteenth century they controlled the principal sea routes from Europe to Asia, through the Straits of Magellan at the foot of South America and around the Cape of Good Hope beneath Africa. For the English these routes suffered from other serious drawbacks. They were long; ships following them took two years or more to complete a voyage to the East. They were dangerous; pirates haunted the coasts and tropical diseases took a heavy toll among the crews. And as a result, they were expensive. Hoping to find a shorter, safer, cheaper route, English merchants remained interested in a northern passage, either to the east beyond Scandinavia or to the west above America.

The search for a northeast passage began in 1553 when a group of merchants and court officials sent three ships around Norway and into the unexplored eastern seas. Two of the vessels never came back but the third, commanded by Richard Chancellor, succeeded in reaching the Russian coast on the White Sea, from where Chancellor travelled overland to Moscow and the court of Tsar Ivan IV, the Terrible. This visit inaugurated a profitable trade between Russia and England but it did not uncover a navigable passage to China. In the next decade another group of merchants attempted to seek the passage in a northwesterly direction; however, the traders to Russia, now organized as the Muscovy Company, had been given a monopoly on northern commerce and discovery, and they used their privilege to block plans for a voyage of discovery. It was at this point that Martin Frobisher appeared on the scene.

Born in 1539, Frobisher was sent as a youngster to live in London with his uncle, a prominent merchant involved in overseas trade. Through his uncle, Martin joined an expedition to the Guinea coast of West Africa in search of gold and pepper. He was only about fourteen years old at the time, but survived a voyage during which intolerable heat and disease killed three-quarters of the crew. Still eager to become a seaman, Frobisher returned to Guinea the next year, 1554, on another trading expedition. This time he was given as a hostage to a tribal chieftain, apparently as a pledge against the sailors' goodwill, but instead of being returned to his ship he was handed over to some rival Portuguese traders who held him captive for several months. Frobisher learned much from these early adventures and went on to become one of the most famous of Elizabethan England's swashbuckling privateers, his name as well known in his day as John Hawkins and Francis Drake.

The distinction between a privateer and a simple pirate was often a fine one. In theory, a privateer held a commission granted him by a recognized authority, the Queen, for instance, or some European principality. Armed with this commission, he was supposed to confine his predations to ships belonging to a designated enemy. In other words, the privateer was a seagoing mercenary. A pirate, on the other hand, was more like a highwayman; he held no commission and attacked anyone he liked. It is possible that during his career Frobisher did not always keep the distinction firmly in mind, since he landed in English jails at least three times as a result of his activities at sea, though he was never convicted. Privateers were financed by well-to-do merchants who took a share of the booty. It was natural that some of these merchants also were involved in the search for the northern passage and that from the ranks of the sea rovers would come a handful of highly qualified explorers. Frobisher himself became interested in the project and, after several times offering his services to lead an expedition, he finally persuaded the Queen to force the Muscovy Company to grant him a licence to go exploring toward the northwest. His principal financier was Michael Lok, an official of the Muscovy Company who was won over to Frobisher's plans. Together they raised enough money to outfit two ships, the *Gabriel* and the *Michaell*, and a small pinnace. The pinnace, not much bigger than a large rowboat, sank and the *Michaell* eventually turned back, but the *Gabriel* managed to carry Frobisher to the shores of Baffin Island, the outer edge of the Canadian Arctic.

When the *Gabriel* returned to England that fall of 1576, Frobisher brought back with him not only news of a western "streyte" but also evidence that precious metals would be found along its shores. According to one account, before leaving Baffin Island Frobisher asked his men to gather samples of the flora and fauna as proof they had been there and "in token of Christian possession" of the country. Among these "tokens of possession" was a piece of black rock. Frobisher presented the rock to Michael Lok, who for some reason decided that this nondescript hunk of stone contained gold. Perhaps he was genuinely deceived; perhaps he was hoping simply to stir up a little support for another voyage. Whatever his motives, Lok had the stone assayed by three different refiners until he finally located one who told him what he wanted to hear—there was gold in the new land visited by Frobisher.

The gullibility of gold-hungry Elizabethans knew no bounds. Not even the Queen herself was immune to it. She gave Lok and his newly organized Cathay Company a royal charter, one thousand pounds, and a 180-tonne ship, the *Ayde*, to lead a second expedition in 1577. The enterprise was now as much a mining venture as a voyage of discovery. Of the 120 crew and passengers aboard the three ships, 30 were miners, refiners, and merchants. The instructions to Frobisher emphasized the search for gold; only secondarily should he continue his probe of the "streyte." Thus, in its modest way, the 1577 expedition marks the first attempt by Europeans to exploit the mineral wealth of the Canadian Arctic. Other voyagers before, and for a long time after, sought a way through the northland. Frobisher and his backers, deluded though they were, were unique in attempting to tap its wealth.

Elizabethan sailing vessels were tiny compared with later arctic ships. The *Gabriel* was only about 22 tonnes, which was small even by the standards of its own day, and may be compared with Sir John Franklin's *Erebus* (308 tonnes) or, more ludicrously, a modern ice breaker (9000 tonnes) or a polar tanker (155,000 tonnes). Yet size was not the most important factor. After all, Roald Amundsen would navigate the Northwest Passage in a vessel of 42.5 tonnes, one-quarter the size of Frobisher's flagship on his second expedition. Rather, Elizabethan ships were ill adapted to arctic sailing by the standards of manoeuvrability and strength. The typical bark of the sixteenth century had three masts. The foremast and mainmast were square-rigged with large courses and small topsails, designed to run before following breezes but not much use sailing into a wind; the mizzenmast toward the rear of the ship was rigged with a triangular lateen sail useful for tacking. However, in stormy northern waters where ships had to dodge massive icebergs or find their way around seemingly limitless fields of ice, these squat vessels must have been awkward to navigate. Furthermore, they were usually merchant ships designed for the coastal waters of Europe. Their plank hulls, caulked with hemp and tar, formed but a thin skin for absorbing collisions with bergs or the pressure of pack ice closing around them.

By the time of Frobisher the science of navigation was no longer the mystery it had been a century before. Sailors could voyage beyond sight of land with confidence that the stars, the sun, and their compass would lead them back again. Pilots could calculate latitude, find direction, and plot a course with reasonable if not complete accuracy. On the other hand, living conditions on board ship were primitive. Sleeping quarters were crowded, dirty, and, on northern voyages, frigid. Fires were lit only in calm weather and washing facilities were nonexistent. Clothing must have been wet most of the time. Water went stale quickly so the men drank beer. Fire protection was a pair of casks kept filled with fresh urine. Walter Raleigh described crews' quarters as "sluttish Dens that breed sickness" but it was more diet than dirt that weakened Elizabethan sailors. Frobisher's men were given daily a half-kilogram of dry biscuit, four litres of beer, a kilogram of salted meat, a litre of pease (a mash of boiled dried peas), one quarter of a salted fish, and some butter and cheese, as well as small quantities of rice, oatmeal, raisins, and nuts. Without vitamins to speak of, scurvy was inevitable if the cruise lasted long enough, while food poisoning also was likely as stores deteriorated in the absence of refrigeration. One mariner summed up the dreary particulars of a crewman's life: "a hard Cabbin, cold and salt Meate, broken sleepes, mouldy bread, dead beere, wet Cloathes, want of fire."

When Frobisher returned to Baffin Island with three ships in July 1577, he spent a few days cruising in search of gold ore before making landfall on Hall's Island (now called Loks Land) at the entrance to the "streyte." With a party of men he climbed to the top of a hill, where they piled up a column of rocks and solemnly named the spot Mount Warwick after one of the expedition's financiers. They looked back as they descended the hill toward their boat, and saw that a group of Inuit, having mounted the hill behind them, were waving a flag and calling out. Timidly, representatives of the two sides met and exchanged presents. But Frobisher could not linger. He was in haste to find a safe harbour for his ships, which lay offshore amid the moving ice. The Inuit followed, wanting to talk further, and when two of them drew apart from the others, Frobisher and another officer approached them and tried to take them captive. Whether or not he intended taking hostages or was simply looking for an interpreter, Frobisher's attempt failed. The two Inuit slipped away, retrieved their bows and arrows from behind a nearby rock, and pursued the sailors back to the boat, lodging an arrow in Frobisher's buttock. Frobisher escaped but the encounter was not over. Seeing their commander in apparent danger, a party of soldiers from the *Ayde* leaped into a boat to come to the rescue. They pursued the natives and succeeded in capturing one man before nightfall ended the pursuit. Unable to return to their ship in the dark, the soldiers made camp and "lay there al night upon harde cliffes of Snowe and Ice, both wette, cold and comfortlesse." The ships spent a fearful night riding out a violent storm.

Reunited the next day, the expedition turned its attention to collecting minerals, both at Jackman Sound on the south shore and where the main mine was excavated on Kodlunarn Island. At the same time no chance was lost to make contact with the local people and question them about the seamen missing since the previous year. On the south shore a skirmish took place when a party of soldiers pursued some Inuit; several of the natives were killed by gunfire and a woman with her child was taken captive. At Countess of Warwick Sound other, more peaceful, encounters were equally unproductive of the missing men, leading Frobisher and his officers to conclude that they were probably dead, perhaps murdered by the Inuit. Suspicion of the local people was so strong that the Englishmen built a fort on Kodlunarn out of stones and cakes of earth to protect themselves against the attack they expected at any moment. Meanwhile, the miners were hard at work. By August 23 about 180 tonnes of rock had been loaded on board and Frobisher, fearing the onset of ice, ordered the expedition home to England with its gold and its captives.

The Frobisher voyages were not the first contact between Europeans and Inuit in Canada's Arctic. After Greenland was settled by Icelanders in the tenth century there was regular traffic back and forth across Davis Strait. The Vikings had a name for Baffin Island—they called it Helluland, Country of Flat Stones—and the birds and animals they hunted there became exotic trade items in Europe. The white falcon, captured on Baffin Island by Greenlanders and exported to Norway, was a valued hunting bird as far away as the Middle East. Indeed, the arctic islands were known obscurely in Europe in the Middle Ages as the Falcon Islands. Other exotica from Baffin included walrus ivory, live polar bears, narwhal horns, and feathers from the eider duck. At the end of the fifteenth century, when fishermen from France, Portugal, Spain, and England began to visit the shores of New-foundland–Labrador, some of them probably sailed far enough north to meet the natives of Baffin Island and trade with them. The Inuit encountered by Frobisher owned metal goods, seemed at home on a sailing vessel, and were eager to trade, all indications that they were familiar with European ships and men. However, Frobisher's contact with the Inuit is the first about which any details remain and unhappily the pattern of misunderstanding and violence is repeated time and again throughout the history of northern discovery.

We cannot know what the Inuit thought of these Elizabethan sailors dressed so strangely and carrying such deadly weapons. Apparently they feared the worst. During one encounter when one or two native men were wounded, they threw themselves from a high cliff into the water to drown rather than trust to the mercies of their attackers; a sign, thought George Best, that "they supposed us be like to be Canibales." For their part the Europeans showed little sympathy for the local people, who were considered treacherous and primitive, filthy in their personal habits and probably cannibals themselves judging by their predilection for raw meat. Dionyse Settle, a passenger on the second voyage, summed up his impressions: "As the Countrie is barren and unfertile, so are they rude and of no capacitie to culture the same, to any perfection: but are contented by their hunting, fishing, and fowling, with rawe flesh and warme bloud, to satisfie their greedie panches, whiche is their onely glorie." Settle and the others were unused to people who did not live in one place cultivating the soil like honest yeomen, but instead roamed about the countryside hunting and fishing, dwelling in portable tents or ramshackle stone shelters. Certainly the disappearance of the five seamen on the first voyage affected all subsequent relations. It made Frobisher suspicious and belligerent, always seeking the upper hand rather than friendship. And the Inuit could not help noticing that of the four captives carried away by the strangers, none returned.

The captives caused quite a stir in England. Frobisher may have intended them to be presents for the Queen; if so none lived long enough to meet the formidable Elizabeth. He must also have intended them as proof that he had reached Asia, and observers agreed that based on their appearance the Inuit were Asiatics from Siberia. So widespread was this belief that in 1579 the Tsar formally protested the kidnapping of Russian subjects! The man taken on the first voyage died soon after arriving in England "of colde which he had taken at Sea." The three captives of the second voyage survived in England for more than a month. They had their portraits painted, dined with the mayor of Bristol, gave a display of kayaking skills in the Avon River, and were interviewed about the geography of their native land. Then, early in November 1577 the man, named Calichough, died, probably of injuries sustained when he was wrestled to the ground by the soldier who captured him. A week later the woman died, of unknown causes, and the infant boy died shortly thereafter on his way with a nurse to meet the Queen.

While the Inuit were entertaining the gentry at Bristol, the principals of the Cathay Company were greedily assessing the results of tests made on the ore which had been brought back. Despite disagreements over exactly how rich the rock was, it was agreed that it did contain sizeable quantities of gold and silver, enough certainly to warrant a third expedition to Baffin Island, or as Queen Elizabeth now called it, Meta Incognita. This time colonization was added to the agenda, along with gold finding and, least important of all, exploration. A knock-down frame dwelling house was sent on one of the ships to serve as headquarters for a colony of one hundred persons—forty "marriners," thirty miners, and thirty "souldiers." A total of fifteen ships would sail under Frobisher's command; of these, three would remain with the tiny colony.

The fleet sailed on the last day of May, 1578. It was the most expensive overseas speculation of the age, the largest expedition ever sent into the Canadian Arctic. It was also a daring gamble on the part of the Cathay Company and its leading partner, Michael Lok. Despite grandiose plans for the future, the company was perilously close to insolvency. After the second voyage it had not been able even to pay the crews and had had to impose a special levy on subscribers to meet the wage bill. After that, the company had spent two thousand pounds building smelters to refine the ore, as well as outfitting the third expedition. As the company sank deeper under the weight of its debts with each voyage, each future voyage was expected to reap the bonanza which would make all investors incredibly rich, and incidentally pay off their creditors.

However, the 1578 expedition was dogged by bad luck from the time it arrived off Baffin Island to find the "streyte" choked with ice. As the ships waited offshore one of them was struck by a berg and sank. All hands were rescued but much-needed supplies were lost. No sooner had the fleet recovered from this tragedy than it was struck by a wild tempest, which lifted the huge pieces of ice and drove them against the defenceless vessels. "Some of the Shippes, where they could find a place more cleare of Ice, and get a little berth of sea roome, did take in their Sayles, and there lay adrift," recalled George Best.

Other some fastened and mored Anckers upon a great Iland of Ice, and roade under the Lee thereof, supposing to be better garded thereby, from the outrageous windes, and the daunger of the lesser fleeting Ice. And again some were so fast shut up, and compassed in amongst an infinite number of great Countreys and Ilands of Ice, that they were fayne to submit themselves, and their Ships, to the mercie of the unmercifull Ice, and strengthened the sides of their Ships with junckes of cables, beds, Mastes, planckes, and such like, whiche being hanged overboord, on the sides of their Shippes, mighte the better defende them from the outragious sway and strokes of the said Ice.

For a day and a half the ships fought to stay afloat in the storm, sailors working feebly day and night with poles and oars to keep themselves from being crushed. At length the winds abated, but they were followed by dense fogs and thick snow.

Straying off course, the ships were swept by a strong current up into Hudson Strait. The strait had been entered on several occasions before this, but no one had sailed through it and it was not well known. Frobisher soon realized that he was not in his familiar strait but in some new passage, which he christened "Mistaken Straytes." The fleet became separated; some of the ships turned back but Frobisher sailed on, convinced once again that he was on the high road to Cathay. Finally the tug of his responsibilities as mine manager and colonizer pulled him back and he returned to muster the fleet and make another attempt at getting into Frobisher Bay. It was generally concluded, however, according to George Best, that the "Mistaken Straytes" was the real passage to the Far East. The original passage discovered by Frobisher in 1576 was considered to be simply one of several channels that ran among the arctic islands and connected with the main strait via deep fiords indenting the southern coast of Baffin Island.

Ice and storm continued to bedevil Frobisher, scattering his fleet and causing some of the officers to suggest they give up and go home. Their commander, however, was determined to reach the mine, or die trying. According to Best, Frobisher prepared the heavy ordnance and declared to his people that if the ships went down they would do so with a mighty thunder of cannon and all hands would be expected to go down with them. Better that than "become a praye or spectacle to those base bloudye and man eating people," the Inuit. (It is interesting that when the Inuit showed the same desperate fear of falling into European hands they were considered ignorant and savage, yet Frobisher's orders seemed appropriate, even noble.) Finally, at the end of July, some of the vessels managed to rendezvous at Countess of Warwick Sound inside the bay.

Immediately everyone set to work to make up for lost time: "Ye Captaines sought out new Mynes, the Goldfiners made tryall of the Ore, the Marriners discharged their shippes, the Gentlemen for exampel sake laboured hartily, and honestlye encouraged the inferiour sorte to worke." After calculating what supplies had been lost in the storms and what was on the four ships which had not yet arrived, the officers agreed it was not possible to leave behind any colonists. There was not enough lumber to build a shelter; it would take too long to construct one of local materials; and anyway, there was not enough food or fuel to support a large number of settlers through a long winter. The expedition did put up a small building made of stone and lime on Kodlunarn Island "to the ende we mighte prove againste the nexte yere, whether the snowe coulde overwhelme it, the frosts breake uppe, or the people dismember the same." The "house" was stocked with small trade items "the better to allure those brutish and uncivill people to courtesie, againste other times of oure comming." Inside an oven was built "and breade left baked therein, for them to see and taste." As well, a crop of corn and grain was planted, Canada's first experimental farm. By the end of August all these preparations were complete and the ships, with 1225 tonnes of ore, set sail for England.

During the third voyage Frobisher and his men had no significant contact with the Inuit, who kept a wary distance, and so they never did discover what happened to the sailors who had disappeared two years earlier. The mystery of their fate remained unsolved for almost three hundred years until, in 1861, the American polar explorer Charles Francis Hall learned a possible explanation. Hall was living in Frobisher Bay and spoke with Inuit there who told stories which gave their version of the Frobisher expeditions. "Oral history told me," wrote Hall, "that five white men were captured by Innuit people at the time of the appearance of the ships a great many years ago; that these men wintered on shore (whether one, two, three, or more winters, could not say); that they lived among the Innuits; that they afterward built an oomien (large boat), and put a mast into her and had sails; that early in the season, before much water appeared, they endeavoured to depart, that, in the effort, some froze their hands; but that finally they succeeded in getting into open water, and away they went, which was the last seen or heard of them." This plausible account is startling testimony to the durability of native oral traditions.

For five years following the return of Frobisher from his third voyage, Michael Lok attempted to find an assayer who would say the ore from Meta Incognita was worth something. Not surprisingly he failed; modern tests have shown the rock to be a form of sandstone embedded with flecks of "golden" mica. The affairs of the Cathay Company were in disarray; without any gold to pay off crews and creditors the company collapsed. Many investors who had pledged their support before the voyage refused to pay up. Lok turned on his commander, blaming Frobisher for the failure of the colony and the worthlessness of the ore. The whole affair ended in sordid recriminations and financial ruin. Lok wound up in prison, the assets of the company were sold to pay its debts, and the ore was broken up for road repairs. Frobisher managed to survive all the adverse publicity and went on to have an illustrious career in the Queen's navy. He was a leading commander in the battle against the Spanish Armada in 1588, harassed Spanish shipping throughout the continuing war, and died storming an enemy fort in France in 1594.

The voyages of Martin Frobisher to Baffin Island were, strictly speaking, failures. No great mineral wealth was found, no open passage to China, no new markets for English goods. However, in the history of arctic discovery, success and failure are not absolutes. Every expedition, no matter how unsuccessful in terms of its own objectives, lifted a little higher the curtain of ignorance obscuring the North. A few more kilometres of coastline were mapped, another inlet searched, another false lead dismissed. The discovery of the North was a long process of trial and error.

After the failure of Frobisher's gold mine, the Arctic reverted to being of interest to Europeans chiefly as a way of getting somewhere else. Frobisher had suggested two possibilities. Explorers following his lead could either venture north up the broad strait of water which lay between Greenland and Frobisher's "Meta Incognita," or sail west through his "Mistaken Straytes."

The northward route was the first taken up. In 1585 John Davis, supported by a group of wealthy merchants and equipped with a royal patent, sailed to the waters beyond Greenland in search of a passage. Crossing the strait that would soon bear his name, Davis came up against the coast of Baffin Island at Exeter Sound, well north of Frobisher's landfall. He cruised south in fair August weather until he rounded into a broad inlet, Cumberland Sound, which had all the appearances of a westward channel. The water was "the very coulour, nature and qualitie of the mayne ocean," whales were plentiful and seemed to be coming from the west, tides were high, and the farther his ships penetrated the deeper the water became. After sailing about 280 km without reaching an end, Davis was forced by adverse winds and bad weather to turn back, but he returned to England convinced he had located a passage.

The next summer, 1586, Davis was back prowling the Baffin Coast, this time with little success. In fog and poor weather he missed the entrances to all the major inlets and ended up well down the coast of Labrador. On his third attempt, in 1587, Davis sailed a tiny 18-tonne vessel up the western shore of Greenland through Davis Strait and into Baffin Bay, reaching farther north than any other navigator before him, approximately to the modern settlement of Upernavik. Returning south, he crossed to Baffin Island and once again probed the waters of Cumberland Sound, still without satisfying himself whether it was a closed inlet or an open channel. On his return to England Davis assured one of his backers, "I have bene in 73 degrees, finding the Sea all open, and forty leagues betweene land and land. The passage is most probable, the execution easie..." However, war with Spain intervened to end all exploration. In the next decade Davis voyaged extensively through the southern hemisphere, but he never returned to the arctic project.

Davis's initiative was renewed in 1616 by Robert Bylot, captain of the 45-tonne bark *Discovery*, and his pilot, William Baffin, after whom their most significant discoveries were named. On what is perhaps the greatest of all the early northern voyages of discovery, these two sailed their ship up the west coast of Greenland past Davis's farthest north to the top of Baffin Bay, a latitude of 77°45′ north. It would be 236 years before another ship would reach this far. Bylot and Baffin crossed the top of the huge bay to the entrance to Sir Thomas Smith's Sound, used by later explorers as the gateway to the North Pole. On their return southward, they discovered and named Jones Sound and Lancaster Sound, before running down the coast of Baffin Island and home. In a single voyage they had identified the three main exits out of Baffin Bay and into the arctic archipelago; and at Lancaster Sound, they had actually gazed into the channel that would prove, many years later, to be the entrance to the Northwest Passage.

The voyage of Baffin and Bylot was a gigantic leap forward in the discovery of the North. Yet their voyage was an end, not a beginning. Papers and maps recording their discoveries slipped into obscurity and two centuries passed before another navigator repeated their accomplishment. Meanwhile, merchants and explorers turned their attention in a different direction, to Hudson Strait and the great inland sea which lay beyond it.

2

Seeking the
Hudson Bay Passage

udson Bay is a
vast inland sea
plunging deep
toward the cen-
tre of the conti-
nent. Most Canadians never set eyes on it—they know it only
as a name associated with a chain of department stores—yet its
impact on Canada's history has been profound. Much of the
bay's 480 000 square kilometres lies well south of what is
commonly considered to be the Arctic. Indeed, its southern
extremity shares the same latitude as Calgary and Brussels.
However, its harsh climate is cold enough to qualify for the
term *arctic* and certainly its northern regions, particularly its
northwest corner, have held a fateful attraction for arctic
explorers.

The bay is entered through Hudson Strait, a seven-
hundred-kilometre channel of swirling currents and treacherous ice, navigable for only a brief period every summer. Once
into the bay, ships face an equally short open season. Around

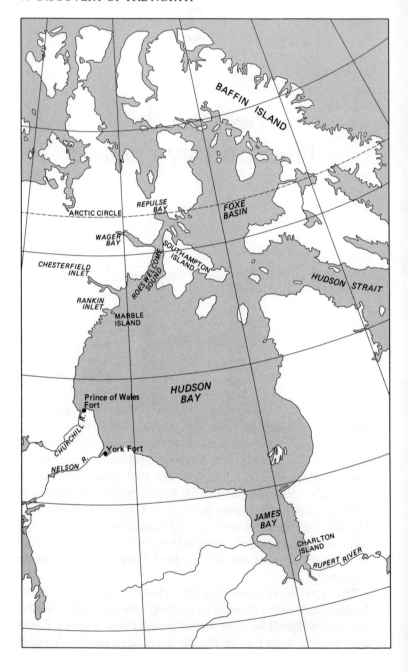

mid-September young ice begins to form close to shore and by November drifting ice pans cover the surface. All winter the bay is swept by chilling winds and driving snow. In the spring the ice begins to break up and sailing can resume late in May, but large pieces of ice continue to move about and threaten a ship's safety. Expeditions penetrating up Roes Welcome Sound in northwest Hudson Bay have encountered ice floes as late as the end of July.

Mariners risked these inhospitable waters because they seemed to offer a way westward through the maze of islands, headlands, and channels at the top of America. We know today that Hudson Bay has no navigable western outlet, but during the seventeenth and eighteenth centuries a series of zealous adventurers convinced themselves, sometimes against all the evidence, that across the giant inland sea lay the pathway to China. And so for about two hundred years the bay enjoyed a virtual monopoly on northern discovery.

The first Europeans to enter Hudson Bay belonged to the crew of the sailing ship *Discovery*, commanded by Henry Hudson, an English mariner, and outfitted by English merchant capital. A passage had long been Hudson's preoccupation but the bay was not his first choice as a likely spot to find it. In 1607 he led an expedition north between Spitsbergen and Greenland, hoping to sail right over the Pole to China. In 1608 he headed northeast beyond Norway but was stopped at Novaya Zemlya, the giant islands off the coast of Russia. Undaunted, he tried again the next year; being once again thwarted to the northeast he sailed back westward, crossed the Atlantic, and investigated the coastline of New England.

Having looked in so many directions with so little luck, Hudson had one last card and he played it boldly. In 1610 he voyaged up the strait that would bear his name. Entering the bay early in August, he pressed the search eagerly southward down the eastern side, reaching the bottom of another large bay (named James Bay twenty years later, after Thomas James, the second European to visit the spot). During the winter the ship's carpenter died, scurvy made its frightening appearance, and supplies began to run low.

In the spring, before the ice thawed, a local Indian visited the *Discovery*. A member of the crew, Abacuk Pricket, described what happened:

> To this savage our master gave a knife, a looking-glass, and buttons, who received them thankefully, and made signes that after hee had slept hee would come againe, which hee did. When hee came hee brought with him a sled, which hee drew after him, and upon it two deeres skinnes and two beaver skinnes. Hee had a scrip under his arme, out of which hee drew those things which the master had given him. He tooke the knife and laid it upon one of the beaver skinnes, and his glasses and buttons upon the other, and so gave them to the master, who received them; and the savage tooke those things which the master had given him, and put them into his scrip againe. Then the master shewed him an hatchet, for which hee would have given the master one of his deere skinnes, but our master would have them both, and so hee had, although not willingly. After many signes of people to the north and to the south, and that after so many sleepes he would come againe, he went his way, but never came more.

This is the first recorded meeting between European and Indian in James Bay. Later Hudson and some of his crew went in search of the local people on foot, but the Indians set fire to the underbrush, apparently to keep the strangers at a distance, and no encounter took place.

When the *Discovery* rode free of the ice, Hudson planned to continue his search for a passage. However, his zeal was not matched by desperate crew members who, perhaps calculating that there was not enough food to keep a full complement alive long enough to reach home, brought a quick end to the voyage by casting adrift their captain, his son, and a few other loyalists in an open boat. On its way out of Hudson Bay the vessel went aground on Digges Island and four sailors were killed by unfriendly Inuit. Two more men died as the *Discovery* crossed the Atlantic, and it was a skeleton crew which finally arrived in England to stand trial for murder.

Skirmish with the Inuit. This record of a hostile encounter between Frobisher's men and the Inuit in Frobisher Bay in 1577 was sketched by John White, an artist and colonizer who accompanied Frobisher on his 1577 voyage to Baffin Island. Later White was involved in colonizing projects in North Carolina and Virginia.

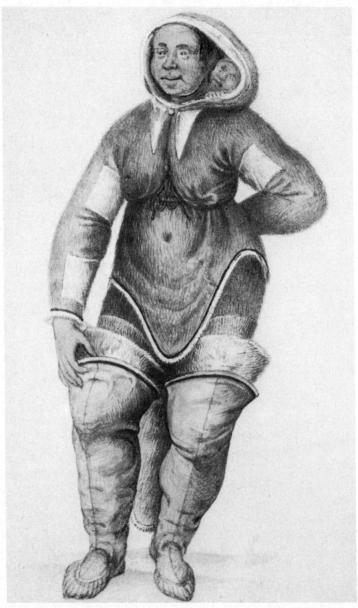

Portraits of the Inuit captives brought back by the second Frobisher expedition, in 1577. Man, woman, and child all died soon after arriving in England. The portraits were painted by John White.

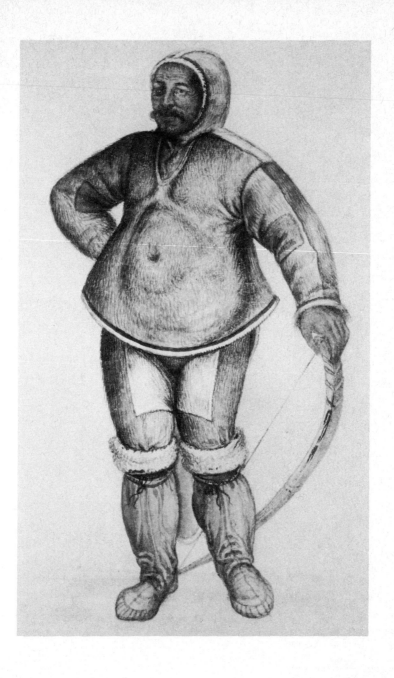

On August 10, 1818, British naval explorer John Ross met a group of Greenland Eskimos as he worked his way through the ice at the top of Baffin Bay. Ross and his companions were apparently the first white people the Eskimo had seen. As for the sailors, they were impressed with the Native dogsleds, later adopted by explorers for long discovery expeditions in the North.
PUBLIC ARCHIVES CANADA # C25238

Early sailing vessels worked their way through the ice pack down leads of open water. If the wind failed, ice hooks were jammed into the floes up ahead and ships were winched forward. When tongues of ice blocked the passage, the men cut through the barriers by hauling on long ice saws suspended from tripods. This illustration shows Captain John Ross's two vessels, the *Isabella* and the *Alexander*, crossing Baffin Bay in 1818.
PUBLIC ARCHIVES CANADA # C119402

When ships passed through Hudson Strait, Inuit from shore would paddle out
in their kayaks and oomiaks to trade. This watercolour by Robert Hood, a
member of John Franklin's first expedition, shows Inuit visiting a pair of
Hudson's Bay Company supply vessels in the strait in 1819.
PUBLIC ARCHIVES CANADA # C40364

This steel engraving, based on a drawing by George Back, veteran of several expeditions along the Arctic coast, gives some idea of what it was like to travel the treacherous seacoast in open boats.
PUBLIC ARCHIVES CANADA # C94116

In July 1821, William Edward Parry was struggling through Hudson Strait on his second arctic expedition when he encountered the Hudson's Bay Company supply ships on their way to the bay. On this expedition, which lasted until 1823, Parry tried to find a Northwest Passage out of northern Hudson Bay, and failed.
PUBLIC ARCHIVES CANADA # C1906

A group of Inuit drawn by Captain G. F. Lyon, commander of the *Hecla* on Parry's second expedition. These natives were inhabitants of the Melville Peninsula, on whose southeastern shore is an inlet named for Lyon.
PUBLIC ARCHIVES CANADA # C25703

As it turned out, the mutineers were never punished. London was more excited by the news of Hudson's discovery than by the fact that he paid for it with his life. A new company was formed, the "Company of Merchants of London, Discoverers of the North-West Passage"; armed with a royal charter, it dispatched two ships to probe the huge bay. The pilot on one of these ships was none other than Robert Bylot, a mutinous member of Hudson's crew. After wintering in the mouth of Nelson River, the expedition returned to report that the western shore of the bay contained no promising inlets and that if a passage did exist it must be farther to the north, up Roes Welcome Sound for instance. The company outfitted three more expeditions but each time the results were disappointing.

Enthusiasm for the Hudson Bay route waned, and all but died completely after news of the fate of Jens Munk and his men. Munk was a Danish naval captain sailing with instructions from the king of Denmark, Christian iv. Danes had recently begun taking part in the whale "fishery" of the North Atlantic and, with this experience to draw on, it was natural for them to be interested in the search for a western passage. In 1619 Munk led two ships up Hudson Strait and into the bay, which he named "Novum Mare Christian." Crossing to the mouth of the Churchill River, the expedition was caught by rapidly worsening weather conditions and forced to pass a horrifying winter. Extreme cold and lack of fresh food claimed the lives of sixty-one sailors. By June of the next year only Munk and two others were alive, but somehow they managed to sail the smaller of the two vessels back to Denmark. This was the end of Danish participation in the search for a passage to China.

In 1631 there were two more attempts to locate a western passage out of Hudson Bay. One expedition was led by Luke Foxe, who sailed for a group of London merchants. Foxe skirted almost the entire western shore of the bay, then penetrated north through the channel and into the basin which bears his name. Nowhere did he find what he was looking for and, taking the experience of Munk to heart, he returned to England the same season.

Meanwhile Thomas James, carrying the standard of the merchants of Bristol, also examined the west coast. He then turned his ship to the south and wintered on Charlton Island in James Bay. The next spring he renewed his search, but it was futile. There was nothing in the bay but an implacable coastline of swamp and rock and a climate that made colonization unthinkable. After a beginning of great expectations, the exploration of Hudson Bay ceased.

For several decades the bay was undisturbed by European ships, and when they returned it was with rather a different object in view. To the south the fur trade was expanding inexorably inland from its cradle along the St. Lawrence River. An alliance of traders and missionaries was spreading French influence up the Ottawa Valley, across the Great Lakes, and down into the Mississippi River country. In 1660 two *coureurs de bois*, Pierre Radisson and his brother-in-law, Médard Chouart, Sieur des Groseilliers, learned from the Indians around Lake Superior of a vast "northern sea" where furs were rich and plentiful. Piecing this information together with what they knew already, Radisson and Groseilliers realized that ships sailing from Europe directly into the northern sea, Hudson Bay, would find themselves right at the heart of the best fur country on the continent. The French authorities were not interested in this plan, so the two adventurers went to England, where a more receptive audience of merchants listened intently. In 1668–69 the *Nonsuch*, with Groseilliers aboard, sailed to the bay and brought back a valuable cargo of furs. The next year, 1670, the Hudson's Bay Company was formed with a royal charter, which gave it a monopoly over trade in all the lands drained by rivers flowing into the northern sea.

A search for the Northwest Passage was one of the things the new company had on its agenda, but it was well down the list. First of all a regular trade had to be established, men recruited, and posts constructed at convenient spots around the bay. None of this was allowed to happen unopposed. The French in

New France were very jealous of this new, sea approach to the fur country and wanted access to it themselves. The two sides fought for control of the bay for many years and during this time there was no opportunity for exploration. Finally, in 1713, under the terms of the Treaty of Utrecht, Great Britain received firm title to Hudson Bay and the English company was secure in its monopoly of trade.

In 1713, the year of the Peace, James Knight became overseas governor of the Hudson's Bay Company. Knight was already an elderly man with a chequered history in the company's employ. He had joined thirty-seven years before as a carpenter and had risen through the ranks to become a post master. But then he'd been charged with private trading, a mortal sin as far as the company was concerned, and he was dismissed. Five years later he was reinstated, to lead an expedition of four ships and over two hundred men against the French in the bay. This sortie was a success and Knight remained in the bay until 1700, when he returned to London and retired from the trade. However, he continued to own stock in the company and was a member of its committee of directors. On September 11, 1714, it was the veteran trader James Knight who went ashore at York Fort, formally accepted the surrender of the French occupiers, and set about rebuilding the trade.

Knight did not allow his advanced years (he was now almost seventy-five) to dim his enthusiasm for taking on new projects. Primed with stories told to him by far-off Indians who came down to York Fort to trade, the governor became convinced that deep in the interior, across the trackless barrens, lay a treasure land of precious metals. His geography was confused, but essentially Knight concluded from what the Indians told him that about 1500 km to the northwest there was a great river, the banks of which abounded with raw copper, "lumps of it so bigg that three or 4 Men cant lift it." Not too many days' travel beyond this "copper river" an unknown group of Indians lived on the shores of a western sea and adorned themselves with a "Yellow Mettle" which must be gold. Knight theorized that a sailing ship could reach these deposits by steering out of Hudson Bay through the Strait of Anian which, though undiscovered, must exist. The hopeful plan was summarized by one of Knight's officers: "I am of a Opinion there is a Considerable quantity of Copper towards those parts; (it being a prodicious way up in the Country) and not capable to be brought down by land; yett if we Can find a Communication by Navigation nothing Can hinder us from so rich a purchass."

Knight returned to England to put his plan before the company. By this time he was retired from the service; what he was looking for was company support for a private expedition. After a winter of discussions he received two ships, the 36-tonne sloop *Discovery* and the 90-tonne frigate *Albany*, manned by a combined crew of about thirty-seven sailors. Knight's sailing directions were "to find out the Streights of Anian, and to make what Discoveries you possibly can, and to obtain all sorts of Trade and Commerce....Especially to find out the Gold and Copper Mines if possible." Contemporary maps showed the Strait of Anian joining the northwest corner of Hudson Bay to the Pacific Ocean. The most promising spot to seek the entrance seemed to be up Roes Welcome Sound and that is where Knight and his vessels headed when they sailed from England in June 1719. It would be fifty years before anyone knew for certain what happened to them.

When the vessels were not heard from at all that fall it was assumed that they were passing the winter in some safe harbour in Hudson Bay, as in fact they were. The optimists even argued that Knight had found his way across to the Pacific. As the summer of 1720 faded into autumn, however, and then another winter came around, fears began to grow for the safety of the expedition. In 1721 orders were sent to the bay to dispatch a search vessel, but it was another year before these orders were carried out. Even then the search was cursory. Pieces of wreckage were found floating in the water by the rescue sloop, whose captain, John Scroggs, concluded that Knight's vessels had broken up on the reefs and that the crews had been slaughtered by local Inuit. This seemed to satisfy the Hudson's Bay Company, which searched no further. Not until the 1760s was the actual fate of the expedition discovered, quite by accident.

Marble Island is a small, surf-battered piece of rock lying about sixteen kilometres off the entrance to Rankin Inlet. On a sunny day the rock appears on the water like a white, glistening jewel. As traders from the Hudson's Bay Company post at Churchill River came north in their sloops each summer to meet the Inuit, they could not help but notice Marble Island and, more importantly, the large number of black whales inhabiting the water around it. In the nineteenth century the island would provide winter shelter for a sizeable American whaling fleet; in the 1760s whaling activity was on a much more modest scale. The Hudson's Bay Company sent a sloop north each summer using the island as a base and cruising the inlets and bays of its ragged shore. During one of these voyages, in the summer of 1767, a whaleboat wandered into a small harbour on the eastern side of the island, where the crew discovered the ruins of a dwelling house and the remains of at least one sailing vessel. Several graves were found nearby. Ironically, Samuel Hearne, who would later embark on his own search for the western copper mines, was among the sailors who discovered this final resting place of James Knight and his men. Hearne returned to the spot a couple of years later and heard from some elderly Inuit their account of the end of the Knight expedition. Apparently the ships had arrived at the island late in the fall of 1719, intending to stay for the winter, and were wrecked in the harbour. (A sunken wreck was discovered there in 1971.) Weakened by scurvy and exposure, the men began to die. With Inuit help a few survived two winters on the bleak, windswept island but by the summer of 1721 only two were still alive. Hearne described what he learned of their poignant deaths.

Those two survived many days after the rest, and frequently went to the top of an adjacent rock, and earnestly looked to the South and East, as if in expectation of some vessels coming to their relief. After continuing there a considerable time together, and nothing appearing in sight, they sat down close together, and wept bitterly. At length one of the two died, and the other's strength was so far exhausted, that he fell down and died also, in attempting to dig a grave for his companion.

With the disappearance of James Knight, interest in northern exploration died also. The Hudson's Bay Company had invested over seven thousand pounds in the expedition, the equivalent of a year's trade. It was not interested in repeating such a dangerous experiment, or in having others do so. For the time being the matter of a Northwest Passage was closed. However, within a decade a new and most persistent enthusiast appeared on the scene to press the search for a passage, even to threaten the company's livelihood in the bay. For twenty years he singlehandedly kept alive the hope that a passage out of Hudson Bay would be found, despite all evidence to the contrary presented by a steady stream of mariners he dispatched to test his theories.

Arthur Dobbs was born in 1685 on the family estate at Carrickfergus, not far from Belfast in northern Ireland. His great-great-grandfather had arrived in the town in 1599, an army officer sent by Queen Elizabeth to pacify the local residents. There had been Dobbses at Carrickfergus ever since. Arthur inherited the family home when he was just twenty-four years old and proved to be a progressive, popular landlord. In 1727 he was elected member of the Irish parliament, where his improving instincts could be applied to the great issues of the wider world. He wrote a book advocating wholesale reforms in the administration of Irish affairs and regularly set down his opinions in long memos for the benefit of the British prime minister. Dobbs was an aggressive colonialist. He saw great advantages in overseas trade and firmly believed in vigorous action to check French expansion in America. Given these interests, it was natural that Dobbs was excited by the possibility of a Northwest Passage and the great benefits its discovery would bring to British imperial trade. If the British did not take the initiative, the French would find the passage and the entire northwest interior of the continent would be lost. Should the British be first to sail through the passage to California, however, Dobbs was convinced of the enormous profits to be won. "By making a few Settlements there we should ingross All their Commerce and open a New Market for our Manufactures vastly Advantagious to us, Inlarge our Trade for furrs, increase our Navigation and Employ all our Poor, and by civilizing those Countrys make Numberless Nations happy..."

Early in the 1730s Dobbs began his campaign to promote an expedition to Hudson Bay to search for the passage. Initially he had trouble drumming up support. The British navy was reluctant to sponsor an expedition which might infringe on the chartered territory of the Hudson's Bay Company, while the company was not very interested in once again committing itself to the unpredictable northern waters of the bay. The company did send a sloop toward Rankin Inlet in 1737, but it was a discouraging venture and Governor Sir Bibye Lake used it as an excuse to deny Dobbs any further cooperation. It was at this point that the search for a passage became an all-out assault on the Hudson's Bay Company.

As far as Dobbs was concerned, the company's original charter required it to prosecute the search. The Hudson's Bay Company was threatening British interests abroad with its obstructionist tactics, unable or unwilling to exploit its own territory fully, yet standing in the way of more enterprising merchants. Dobbs later spelled out the logic of his accusations:

> The Company avoid all they can making Discoveries to Northward..., or extending their trade that Way, for fear they should discover a Passage to the Western Ocean of America, and tempt, by that Means, the rest of the English Merchants to lay open their Trade, which they know they have no legal Right to, which, if the Passage was found, would not only animate the rest of the Merchants to pursue the Trade through that Passage, but also to find out the great Advantages that might be made of the Trade....

Arthur Dobbs was an able propagandist, a man of some political influence, a persuasive debater and pamphleteer, but he was not a seaman. Everything he knew about Hudson Bay he knew from books. He studied the narratives of the few explorers who had scouted the coastline, then gave free rein to his imagination to conclude just about anything he wanted. He was ignorant of the movements of ice, the variations of tides, the severity of northern winters; he fantasized that Hudson Strait was actually ice-free for all but a brief period in the spring and that the Northwest Passage would be found a short distance up Roes Welcome Sound. Motivated by a dark suspicion of the Hudson's Bay Company and an insistent belief in the existence of a wide open passage, he spun his dreams and planned his expedition.

Dobbs was shrewd enough to know that if he was going to mount an expedition with any hope of success he, the arm-chair sailor, needed an ally, a practical man of the sea with experience in the bay. He found such an ally in Christopher Middleton. Middleton was the captain of one of the Hudson's Bay Company supply ships which plied between London and the bay each summer. He had commanded more than a dozen annual voyages, written a scientific paper on magnetism, and knew as much about the company's affairs on the west coast as anyone. Dobbs innocently approached the captain in 1735 to ask for information about the distant corner of the bay which interested him. He discovered in Middleton another believer in the Northwest Passage. As an employee of the Hudson's Bay Company, the veteran captain had much to tell Dobbs about sailing conditions in the bay and the experiences of previous expeditions to the north. The company was very secretive about its activities; Middleton was sharing information available nowhere else.

Middleton agreed with Dobbs that the Hudson's Bay Company was half-hearted in its search for a passage. But seafaring was his only means of livelihood and he was not about to throw in with his new friend unless he was offered a definite commission. Finally in 1741 the call came. Dobbs had persuaded the British Admiralty to outfit two ships to sail to

Hudson Bay, and Christopher Middleton was asked to take command. It would be the first government-supported British naval expedition to go in search of the Northwest Passage.

The larger of the two vessels was H.M.S. *Furnace*, newly built to serve in the war with Spain which had begun two years before. The *Furnace* was a bomb vessel, twenty-seven metres long and specially constructed to carry the heavy mortars used to fire on coastal fortifications. These mortars, weighing several tonnes apiece, rested on thick bomb beds laid below deck, and the entire ship was strengthened to handle the enormous force of the recoil. Strong of hull and broad of beam, the *Furnace* was ideally suited to the dangers of arctic exploration. It was accompanied by the converted coal carrier *Discovery*, brought along mainly to carry supplies. Together the ships carried a complement of ninety men and right from the start crews were hard to find; Britain was, after all, at war. Middleton was able to hire some of his officers away from the Hudson's Bay Company, but for ordinary seamen he relied on impressment and an armed guard around the vessels to prevent desertion. "Besides the Lieutenant and the two Masters," he wrote after it was all over, "there was not a Person in either Ship skilled enough in Sea-Affairs, to have so much as guess'd in what Part of the World he was, without being told." An unhappy situation for ships bent on discovery in little-known waters.

The Hudson's Bay Company was alarmed at the thought of an expedition over which it had no control probing into the secret corners of its trading empire and perhaps opening it up for rival merchants to follow. But the Admiralty asked the company to cooperate and orders eventually went out to the bay that, if called on, post masters should give what assistance they could to the explorers. It was not long before such reluctant hospitality was put to the test. Middleton got away from England later than he intended that season of 1741 and, after entering the bay, decided to go directly into winter harbour at Churchill River. The ships were secured in the river while the bulk of the men found accommodation at the company's original post, abandoned the previous year in favour of the new, stone Prince of Wales Fort located close to the mouth of the river. The derelict old building, in Middleton's words "nothing but a Heap of rubbish," was in need of much repair, which the sailors immediately set to work to carry out. James Isham, master at the post, provided what fresh meat and warm clothing he could and loaned Indians to hunt for the newcomers. But despite these preparations the winter was an appalling one. As the temperature fell, the Indians went away and fresh meat became scarce. The men began to weaken, then develop scurvy. Several had frostbitten toes and fingers amputated. In March they began to die. Before the winter ended, thirteen of Middleton's men were buried at Churchill River. Those who survived were weak and dispirited. When the expedition set sail again at the end of June 1742, to hunt for the passage, fully half of the men could not do their work.

Yet the voyage was actually just beginning. Driving northward through wet fog and heavy ice, the two ships struggled up Roes Welcome Sound, at times so helpless amid the drifting floes that the exhausted crew had to take the tow lines out in rowboats and pull them along. On July 12 the expedition passed beyond the northernmost point of any previous explorers in the bay. On the mainland side a narrow inlet opened to the west and Middleton ducked into it. Might this be the passage? He would have lots of time to find out. For the next three weeks heavy ice from the Welcome was carried into the inlet by wind and tide and the ships could not escape. For a few days it looked as though they would be trapped there for another winter, a terrifying prospect for men already reduced by scurvy and hard work. Neither Middleton nor any of his men actually reached the head of the inlet, which he called Wager after the first lord of the Admiralty, but he saw enough to convince him that it was not the passage which he sought.

When the ice finally relented early in August, the ships slipped out into the Welcome and resumed their survey northward. This was territory no one had explored before; Middleton's excitement must have been intense. Today we know he was heading nowhere, but he fully expected at any moment to see the coastline open and reveal a broad channel of open water leading away to California and the "western american ocean." Instead he found nothing but disappointment.

When he reached the top of the sound, Middleton sighted a prominent headland which he immediately named Cape Hope because of his fervent hope that it was the extreme northern tip of America. But it wasn't. "We worked up round it through much straggling Ice all Night. In the Morning, when the Sun cleared away the Haze, to our great Disappointment, we saw the Land from the low Beach quite round to the Westward of the North, which met the Western Shore, and makes a very deep Bay. Thus our Hopes of a Passage that Way were all over." Middleton reflected his disappointment in his choice of a name for this dead end, Repulse Bay. But he was still faced with a puzzle. All the way up the Welcome he had sailed against strong tides, which seemed to originate from somewhere ahead. If the sound was landlocked, what ex‑ plained the tides? He found his answer in a narrow, ice-choked strait connecting the Welcome to Foxe Basin over the top of Southampton Island. This Frozen Strait, as he called it, solved his puzzle and ended his exploration. The ships turned around and, after a brief survey of the coastline farther to the south, sailed for home.

Later Middleton was criticized for not sending a boat to make a careful inspection of the shore, but the condition of his men has to be remembered. He wrote: "The greatest Part of our Men were not only sick, but had also lost the Use of their Limbs; so that if I had mann'd the Boat, the remaining Hands would have been insufficient to have work'd the Ship, or handled the Sails." As it was he had trouble enough bringing the vessels home, "having not above 3 Men and 4 Officers who did Duty, that were able to come on Deck." When he reached the Orkney Islands in September he was forced to impress another eight or nine men just to get his ships the last leg of the voyage to London.

Middleton's voyage, unsuccessful in terms of its purpose, was nonetheless a great accomplishment. Leading a group of ill-trained, sick, semi-mutinous sailors, the captain made the first thorough reconnaissance of the northwest corner of Hudson Bay and sorted out the complex puzzle of its various bays and straits. Years later Sir Edward Parry would return to this spot and record his admiration for what Middleton had done. He deserved a hero's welcome. Instead he was hauled before a government inquiry, his honesty questioned, his talents belittled, and his career ruined.

On his return to England, Middleton wrote to his old ally Arthur Dobbs expressing disappointment at the outcome of the voyage. "Undoubtedly there is no hope of a Passage to encourage any further Trial between Churchill and so far as we have gone, and if there be any further to the northward, it must be impassable for the Ice, and the Narrowness of any such Outlet." This would remain Middleton's opinion and at first Dobbs seemed willing to accept it. "I apprehend it would be in vain to push it any farther that way," he wrote the captain and broached a new plan which involved crossing the northwest interior with a chain of "proper settlements" all the way to the Pacific. Crucial to this plan, as it was to all Dobbs's considerations, was breaking the Hudson's Bay Company's monopoly. He urged Middleton to collaborate with him on a book which would utilize the explorer's first-hand knowledge of the bay to put the case for free and open trade. But Middleton demurred; he was sympathetic to free trade but Dobbs's plans were in his opinion impractical.

At this point, early in 1743, Dobbs suddenly took a new tack. On close examination of the documents, he concluded, or pretended to conclude, that Middleton had actually discovered a passage without knowing it. "I can almost prove that you were in the Passage," he wrote confidently, "and that Wager River is properly Wager Strait, and not a fresh Water River; and that the Way you enter'd it was one, though not the greatest and easiest way into the Strait." If this congratulatory letter was actually a veiled invitation to join in a hoax to obtain backing for another expedition, Middleton did not rise to the bait. He knew what he had seen; there was no passage. But Dobbs was persistent. He sent his agent to tell Middleton that he, Dobbs, was planning to "lay open" the Hudson's Bay

Company trade in America and would be extremely grateful for a letter from Middleton stating that there was still hope of locating a passage out of the bay. Again the captain refused. He was not given another chance. In the spring Dobbs turned on him, demanding an inquiry into his conduct of the expedition, charging that he had lied about what he had seen and had suppressed clear evidence of the existence of a Northwest Passage.

Dobbs based his case on a combination of armchair theorizing and slander. He argued first of all that in spite of Middleton's report, a passage must exist because all the evidence said it did. In the mid-eighteenth century, when ships lacked any but the simplest instrumentation, mariners depended a great deal on observing natural phenomena such as tides, currents, and animal life. It was commonly believed that Hudson Bay, being so far from the ocean, would have no tides of its own so that if tides were experienced they must come from the west, through a channel. Put simply, follow the tide to its source and you would discover the westward-leading passage. Whales were another telltale sign. It was considered that no whales could possibly make the long journey up Hudson Strait into the bay each season. Since they could not live under the ice, this left only one explanation for their presence in the northwest corner of the bay: a passage through which they swam from the Pacific. Because Middleton saw "whales, Seales and Sea-Horses" in Wager Inlet, said Dobbs, the inlet must be a strait.

Middleton refuted these arguments fairly easily. There were tides all right, he admitted, but they came in at the mouth of the Wager, not out, indicating that they had a source somewhere else, a source he located at Frozen Strait. As for the whales, why did he see them only around the entrance to the inlet and not deeper toward the interior where one would expect to find them if indeed they came from the west? "As for Mr. Dobbs' Seals and Sea-Horses in the River Wager, I take them to be all his own; I never saw any there myself." Yet Middleton realized that his adversary was not really interested in argument and persuasion. "But no Matters of Fact have

Power to convince him; and his Scheme rests entirely upon Presumptions, which all Observations and Experience directly contradict."

Dobbs's charges of personal incompetence cut deeper. It was true that the head of Wager Bay was not thoroughly examined. Middleton saw enough to convince himself that the inlet led nowhere but not enough to remove every shred of doubt. More importantly, on his homeward journey he had failed to dispatch boats to survey the coastline south of 65° north latitude, as it turned out thereby missing a chance to discover Chesterfield Inlet. The captain had good reasons for his conduct. His original orders made no mention of exploring so far south, and his men were too reduced by illness and fatigue to carry out a survey anyway. "But what Freshwatergentleman could ever imagine this in an easy Chair!" Middleton spat in disgust, his patience worn thin. Nevertheless his inability to provide a convincing account of a long stretch of shoreline gave Dobbs an opportunity to insist that here was yet another place that a passage might begin.

Not only was Middleton incompetent, Dobbs argued, he also showed signs of treachery. Dobbs was able to collect several members of the expedition who were willing to state that Middleton had mistreated his men, suppressed information, and lied about what he had seen. These crewmen were probably bribed by Dobbs with offers of jobs in future expeditions; one of them, William Moor, Middleton's own cousin, was later given command of another discovery ship. But why would the commander sabotage his own expedition? According to Dobbs, before Middleton left England he was offered a bribe by the Hudson's Bay Company not to be successful in his search. Dobbs carefully stopped short of saying that Middleton accepted this money and there was no evidence presented that he was even offered it, yet Dobbs concocted a theory linking the captain and the company in a dark conspiracy to hoodwink the public and keep rival traders out of the bay. So great was Middleton's dishonesty, said Dobbs, that he even lied about seeing Frozen Strait, which probably did not even exist. In the face of such arrogant charges, Middleton could only insist that he saw what he saw. "This is the effect of Ignorance," he wrote in exasperation, "or something worse."

Middleton was eventually vindicated both by the Admiralty and by posterity, but the inquiry which cleared him of any wrongdoing was merely the beginning of a long, virulent campaign waged by the former comrades against each other. A stream of books and pamphlets flowed from the presses as both Dobbs and Middleton took their case to the public in the strongest language. More was involved here than simple bad temper. Dobbs was fighting for his cherished dream, the defeat of the Hudson's Bay Company and the discovery of a Northwest Passage. By discrediting the leader of the first expedition, he hoped to prove a reason for sending another. Middleton, on the other hand, was fighting for his reputation, which in the end took quite a beating. When he joined up with Dobbs, Middleton was well regarded as a navigator with wide experience and a modest reputation in scientific circles for his work on magnetic variation. Afterwards, he was all but unemployable. The Hudson's Bay Company certainly would not take him back. Three years after his return from the bay the Admiralty gave him another command, but in 1748 he was retired on half pay and that is how he lived, a man of small means and no reputation, until his death in 1770.

Arthur Dobbs emerged from his public squabbling with Middleton more convinced than ever that the monopoly of the Hudson's Bay Company must be broken and, amazingly enough, confirmed in his belief in a Northwest Passage. By this time Dobbs had a tendency to believe exactly the opposite of whatever the company maintained, arguing that the traders "to deter others from trading there, or making Settlements, conceal all the Advantages to be made in that Country, and give out, that the Climate and Country, and Passage thither, are much worse, and more dangerous, than they really are." But Dobbs was not fooled. In a book published in 1744, *An Account of the Countries Adjoining to Hudson's Bay*, he presented his own theories about the northwestern interior of America. Dobbs stated that, contrary to popular opinion, Hudson Strait was blocked by ice for only a brief period each spring when floes in the many inlets and bays broke up and were carried out to sea; otherwise the strait was easily navigable all year, even during the winter. He also claimed that the climate of the northwest was much more temperate than the company allowed and that inland settlements would thrive. Drawing selectively on Middleton's observations, Dobbs stitched together a convincing argument for the existence of a Northwest Passage, despite repeated failures to find it. In fact, he argued that the west coast of Hudson Bay above Churchill was perforated by any number of passages and that a man standing on a high hill looking westward would see the broad channel leading away to the west. If this direction was followed Dobbs predicted great economic prosperity.

Dobbs's book was an audacious mixture of wishful thinking, ignorance, and deception. It might be taken as the manifesto of a group of merchants and politicians that he now mobilized to carry on the search in Hudson Bay. After the Middleton expedition, the Admiralty was very leery of the persuasive Irishman and his grandiose plans. This left it up to Dobbs and his North West Committee, a mixed bag of noblemen, ecclesiastics, intellectuals (the philosopher George Berkeley belonged), and friends in high places, dominated by a cabal of about thirty London merchants who shared Dobbs's ambition to overthrow the Hudson's Bay Company. In 1745, in response to the insistent lobbying of this group, Parliament passed a bill offering a reward of £20,000 to anyone discovering a passage through the Arctic. It was not difficult for the North West Committee to raise £10,000 from subscribers anxious for a share of the prize, and early in 1746 the committee purchased two ships, the 163-tonne *Dobbs Galley* and the slightly smaller *California*. At the end of May the vessels set sail from England on yet another discovery expedition to Hudson Bay. Ironically, it was the naval sloop *Shark*, Capt. C. Middleton in command, which was ordered to convoy the explorers safely into the Atlantic.

The expedition began badly. Three weeks out from home, a neglected candle aboard the *Dobbs Galley* set fire to a cabin directly above a storeroom containing the vessel's gunpowder.

Fully expecting to be blown sky-high at any moment, the crew panicked. The helmsman, standing right over the blaze, abandoned the wheel and the ship began to career about, its sails flapping uselessly in the wind. The decks rang with the cries of terrified seamen. However, Captain William Moor managed to rally enough help to extinguish the fire and the *Dobbs Galley* regained its course.

After a slow crawl through an ice-choked Hudson Strait, the ships arrived in the bay too late to begin exploring and headed almost immediately for winter harbour at York Fort. The fur traders were reluctant hosts. They naturally disliked the idea of these interlopers, agents of the company's most troublesome opponents, being in the bay at all, let alone having the gall to come begging for a safe harbour. James Isham, post master at York, may be excused for being surly and impatient. However, he allowed the two ships to winter up the Hayes River and loaned what assistance he could in the way of clothing, tenting material, snowshoes, and food.

Unhappily it was not enough. The sailors, forced to camp out in drafty log tents without enough fresh provisions to eat, began to sicken with scurvy, "this foul and fatal distemper." Just before Christmas the first victim died. Henry Ellis, a passenger on the *Dobbs Galley*, described the awful progress of the disease.

> Our men when first seized with it, began to droop, to grow heavy, listless, and at length indolent to the last degree: A Tightness in the Chest, Pains in the Breast, and a great Difficulty in breathing, followed; then ensued livid Spots upon the Thighs, swelled Legs, Contraction of the Limbs, putred Gums, Teeth loose, a Coagulation of the Blood upon and near the Back Bone, with Countenances bloated and sallow. These Symptoms continually increasing, 'till at length, Death carried them off, either by a Flux or a Dropsy.

Before spring seven men were dead. The ships' officers, meanwhile, lived in a hastily thrown together two-storey log house christened Montague House, where the two captains quarrelled incessantly about the division of food supplies among their crews. Finally, in January, Francis Smith, captain of the *California*, and his wife moved in with James Isham at York. All in all it was an unpleasant winter for everyone.

When the ships headed north from York Fort at the end of June 1747, the arguments of the winter continued. Moor wanted to carry out a thorough survey of the western coastline; Smith wanted to spend time investigating the known inlets which might prove to be passages, especially Wager "Inlet." For a couple of weeks the vessels split up. Moor carried out his survey, while a boat from the *California* explored Rankin Inlet. Later in the month the *California*'s men also entered Chesterfield Inlet, the first explorers to do so, but did not have time to venture very deeply into it. When he rendezvoused with Moor, Smith argued that this new discovery should be followed up. However, time was passing and the main objective of the expedition was still ahead, a complete investigation of Wager Inlet; so the ships sailed on. Once again a promising channel was left unexplored and armchair theorists were given an excuse to maintain that a passage to the west might still exist.

On July 29 the *Dobbs Galley* and the *California* swung into Wager Bay to determine who was right, Arthur Dobbs or Christopher Middleton. Anchoring their ships, the men climbed into boats and continued for several days to row up the inlet between its high, rugged shores. Henry Ellis, for one, fully expected to emerge shortly into the Western Ocean. He based this surprising conclusion on the tides, the whales he saw around him, and also on the barren, treeless landscape, since it was a well-accepted fact "that in Countries of narrow Extent, which are either Peninsulas or Islands, there are no Trees, but only a kind of Bushes and Underwood." Imagine his disappointment when the boats came up against the head of the inlet and "we had the Mortification to see clearly, that our hitherto imagined Strait ended in two small unnavigable Rivers." The ships lingered for a week to make certain that no passage led out of the inlet somewhere along its shores. Satisfied at last that it was what it appeared to be, the *Dobbs Galley* and the *California* sailed for home.

It is typical of the whole debate over Hudson Bay and the Northwest Passage that the two first-hand accounts of this expedition should come to entirely different conclusions. One of the authors, a clerk on the *California*, took a pessimistic view. Weighing the evidence, he concluded that there probably was no passage but that the search might as well be completed by an examination of the coast south of Chesterfield. Even if a passage did exist farther to the north, he reasonably argued, better not to know about it "as it might encourage Men of greedy Tempers to attempt it, both to the Loss of Ships and People." Henry Ellis, on the other hand, who happened to be one of the subscribers behind the expedition, was blissfully undeterred by its apparent failure. As far as he was concerned, the simple fact that for so long people had believed in the passage was enough to prove it existed, "for it is an old and true Maxim, that specious Opinions endure but a short Time, whereas the Truth is everlasting." For those who required more substantial proof, Ellis cited the existence of high tides in the bay. "We may consider Hudson's-Bay, as a kind of Labyrinth, into which we enter on one Side through Hudson's-Straits, and what we aim at, is to get out on the other Side," he wrote. "The Tide is a Kind of Clue, which seems to lead us by the Hand through all the Windings and Turnings of this Labyrinth, and if studiously and steadily followed must certainly lead us out."

Not surprisingly, the irrepressible Arthur Dobbs agreed with Ellis. He seemed immune to bad news. Deciding to organize the North West Committee into an actual trading company with a royal charter, he approached the court with his arguments against the Hudson's Bay Company. The monopoly enjoyed by the company was illegal, he said, and if not illegal then forfeit due to the company's failure to seek a Northwest Passage or to colonize its lands. Government officials were more cautious about tangling with the Honourable Company. They listened seriously to pleas that opening the trade to all comers would ruin it for everyone. In the end they were willing to meet Dobbs halfway. He did not get a charter, or backing for another expedition, but he did get a parliamentary inquiry into the affairs of the Hudson's Bay Company. Witnesses were called from all sides; though there was fairly strong public opinion against chartered monopolies in general, the inquiry found no reason to change the status quo in Hudson Bay.

By the time the parliamentary committee made its report in 1749, Arthur Dobbs had dropped out of the debate. For almost twenty years he had devoted himself to the search for the Northwest Passage, anticipating what it would mean for Britain in strategic and economic terms. His preoccupation led him to become the most vocal opponent of the Hudson's Bay Company and its activities in America. It also led him to bribe witnesses, falsify documents, and unashamedly smear the reputations of men whose views did not accord with his own, no matter how broad their experience. In the end even he got tired of the unceasing search for money and favour necessary to keep his dream alive. In 1753 Dobbs was appointed governor of North Carolina, a position which he held until his death a dozen years later.

As for Hudson Bay and the possibility of a passage there, it was left to the fur trade company to pursue the search in its own good time. No one else was interested anymore. During the 1750s and 1760s sloops were sent north from Churchill each summer to trade with the natives and to explore the coastline. In 1762 Chesterfield Inlet was visited once again and this time searched thoroughly. It was the same old story; the promising passage petered out in a shallow, unnavigable river. If a passage did exist out of Hudson Bay it was too far north to be of much use to small sailing vessels working on very tight schedules. The dream of a water passage faded; it was time to try a new approach to the problem of the Arctic.

3

Overland
to the Arctic

In the eighteenth century there were basically two ways to approach the Canadian Arctic. One way was by sea, through the various straits and sounds leading out of the North Atlantic into the unexplored maze of arctic islands. The sea approach via Davis Strait and Hudson Bay had occupied European mariners for two hundred years with little success. After 1750 the British Admiralty and merchant adventurers grew impatient with this route. The Northwest Passage remained undiscovered, perhaps nonexistent, and ships and seamen were needed for the series of wars which engulfed Europe until 1815.

The other way to approach the Arctic was by land, across the barrens beyond the treeline down to the northern seacoast. For years the Hudson's Bay Company had been making inland forays from its posts on Hudson Bay to draw down the

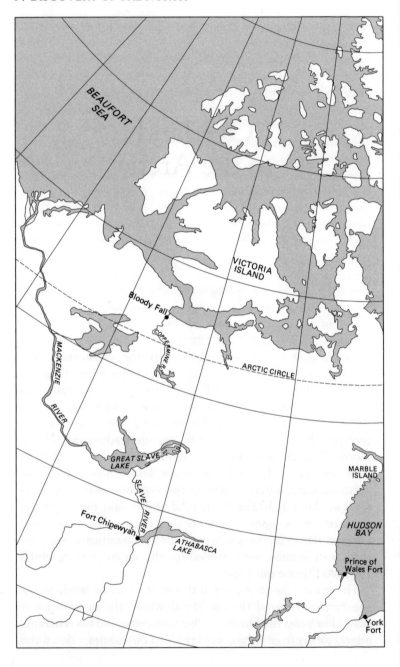

Indians to trade, but company men had never ventured as far north as the treeless barrens. Distances were too great; the way was uncharted; the intentions of the native people were unknown. However, during the 1760s several circumstances combined to overcome this reticence, and the company was persuaded to launch an expedition toward the frozen Arctic.

For decades Indians at York and Prince of Wales forts had been telling traders about the mineral wealth of the northern interior. Rumours of copper and gold had propelled James Knight on his tragic search in 1719. After his disappearance stories continued to be told of "Copper Indians" who picked up ore in lumps from the ground and pounded it into bracelets and headbands. Where these natives lived was not exactly clear. James Isham at Prince of Wales Fort calculated the mines lay about six months' travel northwest of his post. Others thought they were much closer.

In 1762 one of Isham's successors at Churchill River, Moses Norton, sent two Indian men, Idotliaze and Matonabbee, on a reconnaissance mission to scout out a route to the copper deposits. The Indians were gone five years. When at last they returned they told Norton that far to the north "where the sun don't set," they had discovered a broad river bordered by three copper mines. The map they drew on a piece of deerskin showed the coast of Hudson Bay trending directly west to the mouth of this river. As well, the Indian explorers brought back a lump of raw copper and optimistic reports about the fur resources on the shores of this "Coppermine" river.

Moses Norton travelled to London in 1768 to present his new evidence in person to the company committee. Despite the fact that the Indians' map flew in the face of everything a century of exploration had taught about the northwest coast of Hudson Bay, the committee agreed that an expedition should go in search of the copper river. The company was not simply being gullible in its quest for chimerical treasure mines. Furs were its principal interest and it was always ready to investigate reports of unexplored trapping grounds. The company knew that the Chipewyan Indians, who inhabited the forest lands of northern Manitoba and Saskatchewan and southern Northwest Territories, were middlemen in the fur trade. The Chipewyans collected furs from the "Far Northern" Indians who could not be bothered making the long trip to Hudson Bay each season themselves. Company traders felt it was time to leapfrog the Chipewyan intermediaries and establish direct contact with northern natives. This was an objective every bit as important as locating the copper mines.

The man chosen to make the trip was Samuel Hearne. Superficially, he seems an unlikely choice. In 1769 Hearne had been in the company's service only three years. Born in 1745, as a young boy of eleven or twelve he had joined the British navy and seen action in the English Channel and the Mediterranean during the Seven Years' War (1756–63). At war's end he left the navy and three years later joined the Hudson's Bay Company as a sailor, to work aboard the sloop which sailed north every summer from Prince of Wales Fort to trade and hunt whales around Marble Island. It is not known why a junior seaman with limited surveying skills and no experience of inland voyaging was chosen for the copper mine assignment, but it turned out to be a happy decision. Hearne proved to be a strong traveller, quite willing to live off the produce of the land and able to endure long days hiking without food of any kind. Furthermore, the account he wrote of the expedition has become a classic of Canadian travel literature. His sympathy for the Indians exceeded most of his fellow traders' and probably ensured the success of his enterprise. Appalled by many of their customs, he nevertheless believed that undisturbed by contact with the white man the Indians "live generally in a state of plenty, without trouble or risque; and consequently must be the most happy, and, in truth, the most independent also." Hearne recognized that his job as a fur trader was to involve the Indians ever more completely in the business. "But I must at the same time confess, that such conduct is by no means for the real benefit of the poor Indians; it being well known that those who have the least intercourse with the Factories, are by far the happiest."

Hearne's is the name associated with the search for the copper mine but the unquestioned leader of the expedition was Matonabbee, the Chipewyan guide. He set the pace, chose the route, decided when the party would camp to hunt for caribou and when the time was right to move out of the protective cover of the woods onto the barrens. Hearne recognized his dependance; he was more or less a guest and had no choice but to concur in decisions taken by Matonabbee. His admiration for the Indian approached hero worship. According to Hearne, Matonabbee was shrewd, brave, physically handsome, sober, completely honest and trustworthy. "I have met with few Christians who possessed more good moral qualities, or fewer bad ones." As a youngster Matonabbee spent a lot of time at Prince of Wales Fort, even living there for a brief period after his father died. When he grew up he was regularly hired as a hunter for the post. His knowledge of English, combined with mastery of Cree and Chipewyan, made him a useful emissary for the traders to spread their policies among the Indians of the interior.

Before Matonabbee joined his expedition, Hearne made two false starts toward the copper country. His experiences taught him just how necessary a cooperative native guide was. In the first instance, late in 1769, Hearne was put in the care of a Chipewyan hunter who agreed to lead him to Matonabbee, who was away inland at the time. It soon became evident that this Indian, in the words of Hearne, "had not the prosperity of the undertaking at heart." The other Indians who made up the party refused to hunt for food for Hearne and his two white companions. By the end of November they had all deserted, including the chief guide, leaving the Europeans over three hundred kilometres from Hudson Bay "all heavily laden, and our strength and spirits greatly reduced by hunger and fatigue."

Hearne managed to limp back to Prince of Wales Fort and after recovering his strength set off again in February 1770 with a new guide. Once again the expedition aborted. The guide did not seem to know where he was going and was very stingy with provisions. Food was scarce enough anyway; it was not unusual for Hearne to go two days without anything to eat and on one occasion he lived for seven days on "a few cranberries, water, scraps of old leather and burnt bones." Perhaps it was fortunate that in mid-August the explorer broke his quadrant and decided to return to the bay.

To be fair to Hearne's guides, they were probably not as incompetent as he presented them. Indian actions were seldom understood by Europeans, who did not recognize that the natives had a shrewd sense of their own best interests. The Chipewyans did not necessarily want fur traders to become familiar with the interior and the Indian groups who lived there. The Chipewyan position as valued middlemen was best served by European ignorance. Therefore much of what Hearne cursed as dishonesty and stupidity might well have been intentional sabotage designed to keep intruders out of Indian lands.

On his way back to Prince of Wales Fort after the failure of his second expedition, Hearne at last fell in with Matonabbee, who was also heading for the post to trade. Matonabbee agreed to lead the trader to the copper mine, where he had visited several years before, blaming Hearne's previous troubles on the choice of guides and the decision not to allow any women along. According to Matonabbee, this last point was crucial. "Women were made for labour," he explained to Hearne, "one of them can carry, or haul, as much as two men can do. They also pitch our tents, make and mend our clothing, keep us warm at night; and, in fact, there is no such thing as travelling any considerable distance, or for any length of time, in this country, without their assistance." With women doing all the heavy labour, men were free to hunt food for the expedition. As they progressed, Hearne would be shocked at just how brutally his native friend treated women.

On December 7, 1770, Hearne left Prince of Wales Fort for the third time in search of the Coppermine River. He was the sole European travelling in company with Matonabbee and several native companions. Their route took them generally northwest through the scrub forests of the eastern Northwest Territories and then, when spring came, across the treeless "Barren Ground." Initially the party moved at an easy pace. Caribou were plentiful in the woods and there was no need to hurry, since travel in the barrens was impossible until spring. As they marched along other Indians joined them, until the expedition numbered about seventy. In mid-April a halt was called while the Indians dried caribou meat, manufactured tent poles and paddles, and collected birchrind, all in anticipation of crossing the barrens where wood was scarce. Later, as spring progressed, bark canoes were made to be used for ferrying the travellers across the myriad rivers and streams which criss-cross the tundra. By the end of May the expedition had passed beyond the treeline, and left the woods behind them.

Hearne noticed that as they travelled along the Indians were leaving their women and children behind, while at the same time more and more men were joining the party. The reason for this was that the Chipewyan were preparing for war. Indian and Inuit have a long history of conflict along the northern edge of the continent. During the winter the Indians preferred the shelter of the forests, while the Inuit inhabited the coastal areas and the arctic islands. But in the warm season both groups converged on the tundra to hunt the caribou as they migrated in huge herds to and from their calving grounds. All across the North these meetings resulted in bloody conflict. This was not warfare as Europeans knew it; the natives did not carry out sustained campaigns of conquest. Plunder may have been one objective; so may access to favoured hunting places. Other important motives were probably revenge for previous casualties and a desire to prove courage. Some Indian groups believed that the Inuit possessed magical powers which they used to afflict their neighbours with illness and famine, and so hostilities against them were actually campaigns of retribution. Whatever the exact explanation, motives were deeply ingrained psychologically and culturally, as Samuel Hearne discovered when he tried to talk the Chipewyan out of their murderous plans. "But so far were my intreaties from having the wished-for effect, that it was concluded I was actuated by cowardice; and they told me, with great marks of derision, that I was afraid of the Esquimaux." In order to keep the respect of the Indians, on which his survival depended, Hearne had to cease interfering in their plans and could only stand by, powerless to halt the events which were to come.

All through June the travellers trekked westward. A steady downpour of rain soaked their clothing. They slept in puddles of water. Since fire was impossible, they ate their meat raw. Early in July the temperature fell. It snowed and the lakes remained ice-covered. Finally the warm weather came, and on July 14 Hearne arrived at the banks of the long-sought-for Coppermine River. It was a disappointment. The Hudson's Bay Company had hoped to be able to send ships up the river to supply a post and haul away the copper ore. Instead Hearne saw a narrow waterway full of shallows and broken by water-falls, "scarcely navigable for an Indian canoe." He intercepted the river about sixty-five kilometres from its mouth and immediately set out along its banks to follow it to the sea.

Two days later, about thirteen kilometres from the Arctic Ocean, Indian scouts reported that five tents of Inuit were camped across the river not far away. All thought of explora-tion was now set aside as Hearne's companions readied for war. Stripped almost naked, their long hair tied back, their bodies painted black and red, the attackers crept up on the sleeping Inuit under cover of darkness. Falling upon them without warning, the Indians flushed the Inuit from their tents and struck them down in their tracks. Hearne joined the attack, he said, for fear that some Inuit might escape in his direction, take him for an enemy, and kill him. His account of a wounded Inuk woman twined around his legs howling for mercy makes harrowing reading. The Indians killed all the Inuit and plundered their camp, then noticed seven more tents on the opposite shore of the river. Returning upstream to find a shallow place to cross, they descended on this camp as well, but its inhabitants had warning and all but one elderly man were able to escape. The place of this vicious encounter has since been known as Bloody Fall.

After feasting on fresh salmon to celebrate their victory, the Indians were agreeable to accompanying Hearne to the mouth of the river. Again he was disappointed to find the way "so full of shoals and falls that it was not navigable even for a boat." At the coast on July 17, 1771, he found the river entrance blocked by islands and not very deep, and altogether he concluded that "neither the river nor sea were likely to be of any use" to the Hudson's Bay Company. Given the thick fog and drizzle, Hearne did not bother taking observations to locate the river mouth exactly. He was the first European to travel to the American coast of the Arctic Ocean but he seemed unimpressed with the accomplishment, perhaps because he would have nothing but discouraging news to report when he got back. At any rate, he stayed just long enough to claim the coast for the company, then immediately turned south again toward the interior.

Leaving the river behind him, Hearne now went in search of the fabulous copper mines about which he had been told so much. He came upon them about forty-five kilometres south of the seacoast, but instead of the heaps of raw ore he was led to expect he found nothing but "an entire jumble of rocks and gravel." In a four-hour search among the rubble he came up with only one lump of copper, weighing about two kilograms, which he carried back to the bay. Once again the Hudson's Bay Company's hopes for this far northern country were dashed.

Hearne was eager to get back to Prince of Wales Fort, but his Indian guides had a different schedule. First the natives had to rendezvous with their families, which had been left inland when the men went off to attack the Inuit. The pace of travel quickened and for the first time Hearne found himself experiencing difficulty keeping up. His feet and legs began to swell; before long his feet were chafed and bloody, like two pieces of raw meat, pitted with sand and gravel and excruciatingly painful. "I left the print of my feet in blood almost at every step I took," he later recalled. Luckily, as Hearne began to fall behind, the expedition reached the women's camp and he was able to rest and soak his feet.

It was now the end of July and Hearne's mission was complete, but it would be nearly a year before he arrived back at the bay. First he had to accompany Matonabbee and his followers on a winter trading expedition to Great Slave Lake. This trip was not productive of many furs, though, and finally in January 1772 the entire party began the long march east through the snow-filled woods to Prince of Wales Fort. When Hearne arrived there at last on June 30, more than two and a half years had passed since he had set off the first time in search of the copper mine and the arctic coast. With Matonabbee's help he had found both but, as he himself acknowledged, "my discoveries are not likely to prove of any material advantage to the Nation at large, or indeed to the Hudson's Bay Company." Having travelled across the northern wastes to a higher latitude than any other company servant, Hearne seemed to have proved that there was no navigable Northwest Passage leading out of Hudson Bay, and no good reason to settle a post among the far northern Indians. This was evidently the company's conclusion too; it did nothing to follow up Hearne's lead, retiring from arctic exploration altogether for more than half a century.

The journey to the Coppermine was just the beginning of Samuel Hearne's career in America. Two years after completing that assignment he was sent inland to the Saskatchewan River to establish Cumberland House, the Hudson's Bay Company's first permanent trading post in the Saskatchewan country. In 1775 he was recalled from the interior to take over as master at Prince of Wales Fort, and he was there in August 1782 when the French naval commander, the Comte de la Pérouse, arrived off-shore with three ships and three hundred men and demanded the fort's surrender. In 1783, after peace restored the company's possessions, Hearne returned to the bay to re-establish Prince of Wales Fort. He remained in charge there for four more years until ill health forced his retirement. Back in London he continued work on his great book, *A Journey from Prince of Wales's Fort, in Hudson's Bay, to the Northern Ocean*, barely managing to complete it before his death in November 1792.

Of Hearne's companion and guide, Matonabbee, very little is known. After the Coppermine expedition, he continued to be among the most productive traders at Prince of Wales Fort.

Then early in the 1780s, a devastating smallpox epidemic struck his people, the Chipewyan. As many as ninety per cent of this Indian group may have fallen victim to the disease. This epidemic, coupled with the destruction of the trading post at Churchill River by the French, apparently so demoralized Matonabbee that sometime during the winter of 1782–83 he hanged himself.

The same year that Samuel Hearne retired from Hudson Bay, 1787, a young fur trader named Alexander Mackenzie arrived in northern Alberta to take up a position as second in command at a North West Company post on the Athabasca River. Mackenzie was then a young man of about twenty-three years old, a veteran of eight years in the fur business. Born at Stornoway on the Isle of Lewis, Alexander emigrated to New York with his father in 1774 and almost immediately was swept up in the American Revolutionary War. The elder Mackenzie enlisted in a royalist regiment to fight for the King, eventually dying in uniform, and the young boy ended up in Montreal, where he joined the well-known firm of John Gregory, fur trade supplier.

While Mackenzie toiled in a Montreal warehouse, learning the business from the bottom up, great changes were taking place in the organization of the western fur trade. Since first arriving in the Saskatchewan River country late in the 1760s, independent traders from the St. Lawrence, the so-called "pedlars from Quebec," had been waging an aggressive assault on the monopoly enjoyed by the Hudson's Bay Company. Encircling the bay to the south and west, pedlars contacted the Indians right at the source of the furs, saving the Indians a long paddle down to the English posts and suffocating the Honourable Company's trade. As these traders competed with each other for furs, they moved deeper and deeper into the Northwest until eventually, in 1778, Peter Pond crossed the height of land dividing the Hudson Bay watershed from the Arctic watershed and descended to Athabasca Lake.

This pioneering venture opened up a vast new fur country to the Montreal traders, one that led them all the way to the shores of the northern ocean, but it also highlighted a crisis in the Canadian trade. As pedlars advanced farther into the interior it became increasingly more difficult and expensive to transport furs and supplies between their advance posts and Montreal each season. Cooperation among independent traders seemed to be the answer. In 1779 several Canadian trading interests merged into a single company, the North West Company. During the next twenty-five years the North West Company would grow to absorb all its major Canadian competitors, and then engage its arch-rival, the Hudson's Bay Company, in a fierce struggle for control of the fur trade in the Canadian Northwest.

Alexander Mackenzie played an important part in the rise of the North West Company. His initial experience as a western trader came with John Gregory, but in 1787 the North West Company absorbed this smaller rival and, as part of the new arrangements, Mackenzie became a Nor'wester. His first posting was Athabasca, where for one year he was under the command of the legendary Peter Pond. Pond's reputation rested as much on his violent character as on his explorations. He was an arrogant, temperamental man who treated the Indians roughly and was twice implicated in murders of rival traders. But this lawlessness, typical of the fur frontier after all, should not obscure Pond's contribution to the geographic expansion of the trade. His expedition to Athabasca Lake opened a rich new territory which would become known as the "Eldorado of the fur trade." When Mackenzie joined him he was speculating on a much grander breakthrough, an overland passage to the Pacific Ocean.

For a decade Pond had gathered information about the geography of the lands beyond Athabasca from Indians and from his own travels. The result was a map on which Pond drew a large river flowing north out of Athabasca Lake to Great Slave Lake and continuing on to the Arctic, which he called the "Mer du Nord West." In other words, Pond predicted the existence of the Mackenzie River, though he never travelled on it. Then, in 1787, Pond made another map and it was evident that he had changed his mind. On the new map the broad river leaving Great Slave Lake did not flow north. Instead it flowed west, around the top of the Rocky Mountains, which Pond calculated ended at about latitude 62° North, and reached the Pacific on the coast of Alaska. Not only did such a river exist, thought Pond, but it could be travelled in an easy six-day paddle from Lake Athabasca, which he mistakenly placed eleven hundred kilometres farther west than it actually is.

During the winter of 1787–88, Pond's last in the fur country, he shared all this misinformation with his young subordinate, Alexander Mackenzie. Mackenzie made the project his own and in the summer of 1789 he left Fort Chipewyan on Athabasca Lake, heading north by canoe to find the Pacific. Like Samuel Hearne twenty years before, Mackenzie travelled in the company of Indians, for the most part living off game collected along the way. Also like Hearne, he relied on the services of a native guide, a Chipewyan known as the English Chief, who coincidentally was a former follower of Matonabbee. Unlike Hearne, of course, Mackenzie travelled by water, not foot, and the entire trip took only a little over three months compared to Hearne's two and a half years. The first leg of the journey led down the Slave River from Athabasca Lake to Great Slave Lake. Mackenzie was a demanding leader, rousing his small party by 3 A.M. most mornings and keeping them at their paddles until early evening. Great Slave Lake was still ice-covered when they arrived on June 9 and for the rest of the month Mackenzie was icebound in the lake, camping on shore and subsisting largely on fresh fish. With the help of some Yellowknife Indians, the expedition at last reached the mouth of the river Mackenzie was looking for and set off down it, a waterway which no white man had ever travelled before.

For the first few days the river trended generally westward, as Mackenzie fully expected it would. On July 2 a range of mountains "whose tops were lost in the clouds" appeared directly ahead, and for several hours the travellers expected at any moment to be carried over a waterfall or through a rushing canyon. Instead the river swung abruptly to the north so as to travel parallel to the mountains. At this point Mackenzie may have suspected that his route lay more northerly than westerly, but if so he did not confide such doubts to his journal.

Moving easily downriver, he encountered a party of Slave and Dogrib Indians camped on shore. At first the Indians seemed alarmed but eventually a meeting took place. Mackenzie believed they were unacquainted with the fur trade. Almost assuredly they were not happy about strangers coming into their land for they said that it would take several years to reach the river's mouth, that the way was obstructed by many large waterfalls guarded by hideous monsters, and that the travellers would starve for lack of game. These stories did not impress Mackenzie and, taking along one of the Indians as a guide, he continued on his way. Three days later he met a group of Hare Indians and farther on, some Loucheaux. Once again the natives spoke of the perils lying in wait downstream, perhaps the greatest being the Inuit with whom these Indians kept up a running battle and about whom they told frightening stories.

On July 10, Mackenzie reached the beginning of the huge delta now bearing his name. Taking observations to record his latitude, he discovered that he was well north of 67 degrees, a finding which confirmed that he was certainly not on a course for the Pacific. "I am much at a loss here how to act," he wrote, "being certain that my going further in this Direction will not answer the Purpose of which the Voyage was intended, as it is evident these Waters must empty themselves into the Northern Ocean." Mackenzie decided to push on "as it would satisfy Peoples Curiosity tho' not their Intentions," but he had a hard time convincing his Indian companions to follow him. They knew the body of water ahead as "White Man's Lake," probably referring to Russian traders far to the west, and they feared to go there because of the hostile Inuit who inhabited its shores. But the Indians were persuaded when Mackenzie promised to turn back if the river mouth was not reached within seven days.

Following a meandering route through the low islands of the delta, Mackenzie's party came on July 12 to what is now called Garry Island, one of the outer islands which fringe the seaward side of the delta. There progress was blocked by ice and the expedition camped. As Mackenzie looked out across the ice-covered expanse of water stretching away to the horizon, he as yet did not realize that he was only the second white man to reach the central coast of the Arctic Ocean. Might it not simply be another lake, like Great Slave Lake for instance? The Indians had certainly created this impression and there was nothing evident to the eye to contradict them. However, over the next few days Mackenzie experienced the ebb and flow of the tide in front of his campsite and also saw some beluga whales, so that the knowledge of where he was at last came clear to him.

Throughout the delta Mackenzie saw evidence of Inuit occupation; on July 16 he embarked on the return trip still hoping to meet some of these people. But if they were there, they kept hidden and the explorer never did get a chance to interview the true inhabitants of the region. As they proceeded upriver against the current, the going was often difficult. Whenever the wind was favourable, sails were hoisted. Otherwise canoes were towed by men walking along shore hauling on long lines. Stone beaches made for hard walking; at one point the Indians were wearing out a new pair of leather moccasins every day.

As the expedition laboured slowly upstream, Mackenzie received garbled accounts from local Indians of another large river across the mountains far to the west. Presumably this was the Yukon, and Mackenzie concluded that it was the westward-flowing river he sought so avidly. All along the homeward route he sought information from the Indians about this waterway, even trying to hire a guide to take him to it. Mackenzie's enthusiasm apparently was not shared by his Indian companions, who he began to suspect were withholding information from him in order to hasten the end of the expedition. On August 13, Mackenzie and the English Chief had an angry shouting match in which the explorer accused his guide of sabotaging attempts to locate the distant river. The argument ended with the Indians refusing to go any farther. Mackenzie quickly realized he "could not well do without them" and persuaded the English Chief to re-embark. The rest of the trip passed without incident and in mid-September the canoes arrived back at Fort Chipewyan.

Both Mackenzie and his employer, the North West Company, were disappointed at his failure to reach the Pacific. "My Expedition is hardly spoken of," he wrote his cousin after a visit to the summer rendezvous at Lake Superior, "but this is what I expected." He did claim some credit for proving once again that no navigable water passage existed south of the Arctic Ocean, "and I believe it will generally be allowed that no passage is practicable in a higher latitude the Sea being eternally covered with Ice." However, this discovery was a rather paltry consolation prize. In the future, of course, traders and settlers would pour down Mackenzie's river as it emerged as the main avenue of traffic into the far northwest. But in the short term no one followed in Mackenzie's footsteps.

Alexander Mackenzie's voyage to the Arctic in 1789 hinted at his resourcefulness as an explorer. Four years later this promise was confirmed when he made his celebrated overland trek across the Rockies to the Pacific. Once again Mackenzie's accomplishment was diminished somewhat by the fact that the route he pioneered was of little use to the fur trade. Nevertheless, Mackenzie's travels earned him a reputation as one of the ablest trader-explorers of his day. Among his fellow Nor'westers he enjoyed enormous respect and became the spokesman of the wintering partners in their dealings with the Montreal end of the business. In 1799 he resigned from the North West Company after a heated difference of opinion with the leaders of the firm. Retiring to London to nurse his hurt feelings, Mackenzie returned to Canada the next summer to add his prestige to the XY Company, a new concern based in Montreal formed to challenge the North West Company. From that point the upstart company was known as Alexander Mackenzie and Co., and for four years the Northwest was the scene of fierce, often violent, competition for control of the

Canadian trade. When finally, in 1804, the two rivals made peace, Mackenzie retired from the trade for good.

The expeditions of Samuel Hearne and Alexander Mackenzie form a separate chapter in the history of arctic exploration. Earlier, and later, expeditions sought a passage across America and were highly organized in their purpose. Hearne and Mackenzie were first of all traders; explorers only secondarily. Their mission was to seek new trading routes and "undiscovered" Indian tribes. If they also found out something useful about the geography of the North, well and good, but this was not their main purpose. Looked at from the perspective of the fur trade, their expeditions were noble failures. Both men were looking for things which did not exist: Hearne for the rich copper mines and Mackenzie for the westward-flowing river. Not only did these objectives turn out to be imaginary, but the lands visited by Hearne and Mackenzie did not seem productive of furs, or anything else of value, and the fur trade companies did not bother to persist in either direction.

Looked at from the perspective of exploration, however, both men made exciting discoveries, touching down at two distant points along a coastline completely unknown to Europeans. Armchair theorists had to admit now that there was no easy Northwest Passage to the temperate latitudes. For the first time the top of America could be fixed, however tentatively, on the maps of the world. Perhaps more importantly, both men, but especially Hearne, pioneered a way of travelling in the North, one that utilized native knowledge and native technology and relied on local food resources for subsistence. Small expeditions, lightly burdened with supplies, guided by Indians and living off the land as they moved along; this was the example set by Hearne and Mackenzie and in the next century many explorers would follow it.

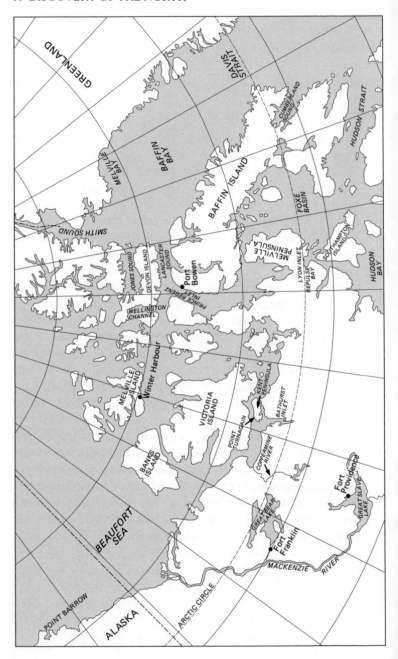

4

The Royal Navy
in the North

When peace settled over Europe following the Napoleonic Wars, the British navy found itself overmanned and underemployed. During more than ten years of warfare the navy had dominated the high seas, blockading French ports, breaking the counter-blockade thrown up by Napoleon, and keeping open the channels of commerce and communications which ensured a British victory in the long run. In 1809, at the height of the conflict, the Royal Navy numbered 773 ships, commanded by 4444 officers, and manned by about 140,000 sailors. Then, in 1815, peace broke out and there was simply nothing for so many ships and men to do. Vessels were mothballed and sailors were sent back to civilian life. In 1818 the Admiralty needed only 121 commissioned ships and about 19,000 crewmen. Ordinary seamen made the transition easily enough; most of them had been pressed into service in the first place and welcomed a return to their former employments. Officers, however, were a different matter. The navy was their career and, even though they were not needed, they could not be laid off. In fact, as the war drew to a close the Admiralty hurried to promote many officers so that they would qualify for higher rates of pay when the employment crunch came. As a result, for every officer in the 1818 navy, there were only three and a half ordinary seamen to command, and fully eighty per cent of the commissioned ranks had no ships on which to serve, no duties to perform.

It is no accident, therefore, that a new enthusiasm for arctic exploration seized the British Admiralty after 1815. What better way to employ idle manpower than in the search for the Northwest Passage? No new discoveries had been made since the travels of Hearne and Mackenzie. It was time to follow up the tentative probings of the eighteenth century with a full-scale assault on the North.

The arctic project no longer had commercial motives. Frobisher, Hudson, Middleton, and the rest had sought a navigable route to Cathay in order to open a trade in spices, silks, and precious gems. At the time, Spanish and Portuguese mariners controlled the southern sea lanes and the British were anxious to discover their own northern passage. But by the nineteenth century the British merchant marine roamed freely across all the world's oceans and had no need of a difficult northern route to China. Instead the search for a passage was now rationalized as an entirely disinterested scientific enterprise carried out solely to extend human knowledge of the world. The project was "one of the most liberal and disinterested that was ever undertaken," observed John Barrow, second secretary to the Admiralty, "and every way worthy of a great and prosperous and an enlightened nation; having for its primary object that of the advancement of science, for its own sake, without any selfish or interested views."

Undeniably there was some truth in Barrow's boast. The postwar period was marked by a revived enthusiasm for scientific achievement, one of the results of which was the proliferation of geographical societies in European capitals. But it was also true that on the northwest coast of America the Russians were conducting an energetic fur trade and apparently preparing to extend their influence around the top of Alaska toward the Arctic coast. International rivalry and national prestige also played their part in the renewed interest in northern discovery. As John Barrow frankly put it: "It would be somewhat mortifying if a naval power but of yesterday [i.e., Russia] should complete a discovery in the nineteenth century, which was so happily commenced by Englishmen in the sixteenth."

While there had not been any official exploration in the waters north of sixty degrees for many years, European whalers had been cruising Davis Strait and the North Atlantic every summer and in the process accumulating a vast store of knowledge about ice, tides, and currents. Whaling in Canada's Arctic began on a small scale in the seventeenth century when ships from Holland and Great Britain hesitantly made their way around the bottom of Greenland and began feeling their way up into Davis Strait. By the eighteenth century the industry was well established, as many as 150 vessels making the voyage each summer. When the Admiralty began to contemplate northern expeditions, it naturally drew on the experience of the whaling men. In 1816 and 1817, reports gathered from these veteran sailors were especially encouraging. Northern ice sheets were breaking up at an unprecedented rate, large breakaway pieces floating southward and leaving seas more open for navigation than at any time in recent memory. Apparently an opportunity existed which the Admiralty could not ignore if it was serious about the arctic project.

At the Admiralty, John Barrow was the chief proponent of northern exploration. Barrow was one of the most prominent public figures of his time in England. The son of a humble Lancashire farmer, he managed by attaching himself to distinguished patrons to work his way into a position of great influence in the public service. In 1803 he was appointed one of the two secretaries at the Admiralty in charge of administering naval affairs. He served almost without interruption until his retirement in 1845, a period which saw the British navy engage in a wide range of geographic discoveries and surveys all over the world. Barrow was also a prolific and popular writer. His books about China and South Africa, both countries he visited as a junior member of diplomatic missions, did a great deal to bring these unknown places to the attention of the British public, as well as to establish Barrow as a minor literary figure. Later in his career he wrote histories of arctic exploration, popular biographies, and, in 1831, probably his most popular work, *The Mutiny on the Bounty*, an account of a mutiny aboard a British ship in 1789. In his mid-teens Barrow spent a single summer aboard a North Atlantic whaler. Despite the fact that this was the total of his arctic experience, he adopted the arctic project as his own—it was, he said, "almost the only interesting discovery which remains to be made in geography"—and he was never reluctant to criticize navigators who failed to achieve in practice what he was convinced must be possible in theory.

One of Barrow's most closely held beliefs was in the existence of an open Polar Sea. This notion was not original with him; it had a lineage stretching back several centuries and by Barrow's time was hotly disputed. According to this theory, the top of the globe was capped not with a massive ice sheet but instead by a circumpolar expanse of open water. The ice seen by whalers and explorers in the high latitudes did not extend all the way to the pole; it was a barrier only, and once sailing vessels pierced it they would have clear sailing across the top of the world.

To test this theory, and to renew the search for a Northwest Passage, Barrow planned a dual expedition. Two ships would sail directly north between the island of Spitsbergen and Greenland, attempting to breach the ice barrier and reach the pole, while another two ships would take a more conventional route to the northwest through Davis Strait. The former, commanded by Captain John Buchan, were battered by ice and storm and had to retreat home without accomplishing much of anything. The latter ships, however, made a pioneering voyage into the eastern arctic, returning great stretches of coastline to the map, opening up valuable new hunting grounds to European whalers, and stirring up one of the bitterest controversies in the history of arctic discovery.

The northwest expedition was led by John Ross, a red-haired Scot who had entered the Royal Navy in 1786 at age nine and had spent most of his years since at sea. Ross accepted his new command late in 1817 and hurried to London to oversee the outfitting of his ships, the 350-tonne *Isabella* and the 230-tonne *Alexander*. These were merchant vessels, chosen for their capacious storage room, and had to be prepared in the usual manner for arctic sailing. First of all the hulls were covered with a mixture of animal hair and tar to form a watertight skin. Then they were "doubled" with a second layer of oak planks, 75 mm thick and bolted in place. Bows were sheathed in iron plate and interiors were strengthened with stout beams and timbers, to absorb the pressure of the pack ice. Flues were constructed to carry warm air from galley fires to the various cabins below decks. Along with a complement of ninety men Ross was provided with an astronomer, Captain Edward Sabine, and an Inuit interpreter, John Sackhouse, a native of Greenland.

The ships got away late in April 1818, and after stopping in the Shetland Islands, where a fiddler was added to the crew, they set off across the Atlantic. It was customary on voyages from Britain to the Canadian Arctic to follow approximately the fifty-eighth parallel of latitude so as to arrive well south of Greenland's southern tip, where ice conditions were notoriously bad. By the end of May, as the ships approached this landmark, icebergs had become plentiful, the temperature rarely climbed above freezing during the day, and the rigging and decks were covered with a slippery coating of ice. Though navigation was difficult, Ross was struck by the awesome beauty of the giant bergs which swept past his ships. "It is hardly possible to imagine any thing more exquisite than the variety of tints which these icebergs display," he wrote. "By night as well as by day they glitter with a vividness of colour beyond the power of art to represent. While the white portions have the brilliancy of silver, their colours are as various and splendid as those of the rainbow..."

As they made their way slowly into Davis Strait, the *Isabella* and *Alexander* were following a route long known to the whalers who frequented these waters. They had learned from a century of experience that early in the season the western side of Davis Strait invariably is blocked by ice borne south in a steady stream on a cold current bound for the Atlantic. In the spring the ice cover in the many channels and inlets of the eastern archipelago breaks up into innumerable pieces; these are carried down into southwestern Baffin Bay, where they congregate into a solid ice plain which the whalers called the "middle pack." Gradually this field of ice leaks down Davis Strait, and Baffin Bay clears sufficiently to allow navigation. However, the whalers could not afford to lose time waiting. Instead they followed a warmer current that flowed up the eastern side of the strait along the coast of Greenland, opening a corridor of water which ships could follow northward to the whaling grounds.

Throughout June the two "discovery ships" joined the whalers as they worked north in the shadow of Greenland's looming shore. Even here the ice was unusually thick in 1818 and progress was bought at the cost of great labour. When the wind died either the bulky ships had to be towed with the boats or, if the pack was close, hooks were embedded in the ice ahead and the vessels were warped along by crewmen sweating over a capstan. Often the way was blocked by narrow extensions of ice which had to be sawed through to allow the ships passage into the clear water beyond. For several days at a time the explorers and their whaling companions could make no progress at all and had to tie up to grounded icebergs while they waited impatiently for the ice to open.

Hugging the Greenland coast, Ross inched his way northward. At the end of July he passed beyond 75° North latitude into a region at the top of Baffin Bay seldom penetrated by whalers. Consequently, the animals were spouting all around. "The number of whales around us this day was beyond any thing we had seen before," wrote Alexander Fisher, surgeon on the *Alexander*. "It being calm, the noise of their blowing resembled the sound of distant artillery.... Sometimes a dozen of them might be seen at once . . ."

The ships now swung to the west across Melville Bay and began perhaps the most dangerous part of the entire voyage. Melville Bay is a broad dish of water overarching the top of Baffin Bay. Its shore is edged with rocky islands and the water is shallow, so the ice tends to gather thickly and hold tenaciously. Between the pieces packed tightly into the bay and the "middle pack" to the south, leads of water open which can be followed to the west. But, as Ross discovered, much depends on the wind. When it blows from the north the sea ice shifts away from the shorefast ice and ships can squeeze between them. A breeze from the south, on the other hand, drives the two packs relentlessly together, grinding into pieces whatever comes between them. In the years ahead, as whalers followed Ross's lead across the top of the middle ice, this 240-km passage would become known as "The Breaking-Up Yard" because so many wooden ships were crushed and sent to the bottom by the shifting packs.

Ross was lucky. Certainly conditions were anything but ideal. Dense fogs froze on the rigging to the thickness of a man's arm. Giant bergs crashing through the pack threatened to overwhelm the ships. It was tedious to have to smash through the young ice which formed each night in front of the vessels. But, on the whole, Ross was spared the worst that Melville Bay has to offer and managed to work his way safely across to the "west water," the curious polynia at the mouth of Smith Sound which remains unfrozen throughout the year. On the way he and his men became the first Europeans to meet the Etah Eskimos. These people, inhabiting the Thule area of west Greenland, appeared on the ice beside the ships full of wonder and initially very timid. According to Ross, they could not believe that he had come from the south, a region they assumed was an icy waste. Apparently they had not seen sailing ships before, believing at first that they were great birds with huge white wings. Eventually the Eskimos, who had come out from the land on dogsleds, were coaxed on board and introduced to the various items of trade the explorers had brought with them, including umbrellas, mirrors, needles, and woollen clothing. But more impressive to the Europeans than anything they themselves had to offer was the sight of the native dogsleds, capable of carrying heavy loads over great distances of ice and snow. In the years ahead British naval explorers would use this piece of Inuit technology to survey thousands of kilometres of arctic coastline.

So far Ross was following in the track of William Baffin and Robert Bylot's great voyage of 1616. These two early mariners also sailed up the coast of Greenland and across Melville Bay, emerging on the other side to find three different inlets leading away north and west into the archipelago, possibly passages, possibly not. Ross's purpose when he arrived in the "west water" was in part to duplicate the discoveries of Bylot and Baffin. Had they located at least one Northwest Passage, or were Smith, Jones, and Lancaster sounds all dead ends? On August 19, the *Isabella* and *Alexander* arrived off Smith Sound. Unhappily, Ross's view was obscured by poor weather and the entrance to the strait was blocked by ice. Nevertheless, based on the lack of pronounced tides or strong currents, he concluded, erroneously as it turned out, that there was probably no opening at the top of Baffin Bay. Even if there was, he thought, "it must for ever be unnavigable." Turning south, the ships passed across the entrance to Jones Sound, and Ross drew the same conclusion: it was a closed inlet. With two possible passages eliminated, and time slipping away, Ross hurried south to investigate Lancaster Sound.

John Ross accomplished a great deal on his 1818 voyage. He brought the Etah Eskimos to the attention of the world, he opened up valuable new whaling grounds, and he re-explored the northern contours of Baffin Bay. However, unhappily for his subsequent reputation, what is best remembered about Ross are his mistakes, especially the one he made in Lancaster Sound. The expedition rounded into the sound full of hope. The sea was remarkably free of ice, soundings showed the water to be deep, and the passage was many kilometres wide with no appearance of obstructions ahead. "It certainly has more the appearance of being the entrance of the wished-for straits than any place we have yet seen," Alexander Fisher wrote in his journal.

As they proceeded up the sound, the *Isabella* ploughed ahead of its slower companion. Early on the morning of August 31, Ross was summoned on deck where, through a thick fog, he saw what he later described as "a high ridge of mountains, extending directly across the bottom of the inlet." Apparently Lancaster Sound was not the passage after all. Ross did not come about immediately, however. About noon an officer in the crow's nest confirmed that there was land ahead. Then, at three that afternoon, the fog briefly cleared and Ross again "distinctly saw the land, round the bottom of the bay, forming a connected chain of mountains with those which extended along the north and south sides." He called these peaks the Croker Mountains, after the first secretary of the Admiralty. At this point no one objected to the captain's order to turn back; the other officers apparently no longer believed that the sound led anywhere. The *Isabella* fell in with the slow-moving *Alexander*, whose crew had seen nothing, and the two ships continued south down the coast of Baffin Island and then back to England, where they arrived in November.

We know today that the Croker Mountains do not exist. They were an embarrassing *trompe l'oeil*, probably the result of thick weather and light refraction that distorted the extent of quite natural-sized ice pieces. But even before they were disproven beyond any doubt, the mountains were the subject of much disbelief and dispute in England. Leading what amounted to a personal attack on John Ross was John Barrow, whose disappointment at the failure of the expedition soured his opinion of its leader beyond any hope of reconciliation. Like Arthur Dobbs in the previous century, Barrow was an armchair theorist with a short temper and a vicious pen. When Ross published his account of the voyage early in 1819, Barrow was unsparing in his criticism. In a scathing review of the book he questioned Ross's seamanship, his intelligence, and his courage. The brunt of the argument was that the commander should have persevered until he had proved beyond any doubt that the mountains existed. Ross took no risks, claimed Barrow, and "knows no more, in fact, than he might have known by staying at home"; the entire expedition was just "a voyage of pleasure." Some of the officers on the expedition joined the dispute, claiming that they had not seen the mountains and suggesting that Ross had acted without proper consultation. Prominent among these was Edward Sabine, the expedition's astronomer. There is no question that Sabine, at the time, did not believe that Lancaster Sound offered a passage westward and argued that Cumberland Sound was a much more likely location. However, during the homeward voyage he apparently changed his mind, and he added a pamphlet to the controversy in which he rebuked his commander for not taking more time to verify what he saw, though he stopped short of saying that he was mistaken. This from a man who had advocated all along they not bother with Lancaster Sound at all!

Ross's self-defence was reasoned and for the most part temperate. As it turned out, of course, he was wrong, but the incident should not be allowed to blacken his entire character. Given that he thought he saw his way blocked, what should he have done? His critics said he should have sailed on. But Ross was under orders and time was pressing. He had been told to watch for strong currents, and in Lancaster Sound there were none. He had been told to concentrate his search in about 72° North latitude, well south of the sound. He had been told to depart for home on October 1 at the latest, so in a limited period of time he still had a large area to search. Furthermore, learned opinion, including Edward Sabine's, placed a possible passage farther south, so he was naturally anxious to continue the search where there was the greatest likelihood of success. Lancaster Sound was eventually discovered to be the entrance to a Northwest Passage after all. But under the assumptions Ross was working with it was very much a secondary objective, and he naturally did not want it to distract him from his main purpose.

All these explanations did not satisfy John Barrow. The

public exchange of abuse ended, but privately Barrow continued to disparage Ross. Just before his death thirty years later
Barrow would dismiss the Croker episode as "a pitiable excuse
for running away home." Meanwhile he was a powerful
administrator with a great deal of influence over postings and
promotions in the navy. The Admiralty assured Ross that he
enjoyed its full confidence, but Barrow worked energetically to
see that the explorer was denied another command. Ross
retired to his imposing Scottish castle to brood and hatch
further plans for arctic discovery.

John Barrow wasted no time putting the existence of the
Croker Mountains to the test. Immediately, he organized a
second northern expedition, which sailed from England in
May 1819. For his commander Barrow chose Lieutenant
Edward Parry, a twenty-eight-year-old officer with sixteen
years' naval experience in the Baltic and North Atlantic.
During the previous year's expedition Parry commanded the
Alexander, second in command to Ross, and in the quarrel-
some aftermath he sided with Barrow in doubting the compe-
tence of his superior officer. Parry was given two ships, the
340-tonne *Hecla* and a smaller brig, *Griper*, with a total
complement of ninety-four crewmen and provisions to last
two years. Among the foodstuffs packed on board were hundreds of tins of canned meat and vegetables, an innovation
which probably did more to ensure the safe return of the
expedition than any decision taken by its leader.

The traditional diet aboard an eighteenth century British
naval vessel consisted of three staples—beer, biscuit, and meat.
Water was impossible to keep fresh, especially on long, southern voyages, so thirsty sailors received a daily ration of beer or
spirits. Flour was served in the form of ship's biscuit, rock hard
and commonly infested with weevils and maggots. As for
meat, it was salted and stored in barrels of brine where it got
tougher and tougher as the voyage progressed. During the
Napoleonic Wars this diet was transformed by the introduction of canning. The process was pioneered in France, where
the navy was supplied with meat preserved in champagne
bottles as early as 1807. Two enterprising Englishmen, John

Hall and Brian Donkin, adapted the process for tin cans and opened the world's first canning factory in 1812. With a nod to its French source the new product was called *bouilli*, which eventually was transmuted into bully beef. Because it was expensive it did not penetrate the regular consumer market for several years, but naval ships were supplied with canned goods almost immediately. Vessels could now range over great distances, remaining at sea for many months, even years, without their food supplies spoiling and their crews sickening. John Ross had taken canned goods on his expedition but, since he had not over-wintered, their worth had not been tested. It was Parry's experience that showed just how thoroughly canning would revolutionize arctic discovery.

Parry's objective was to investigate whether Baffin Bay was actually landlocked, as Ross had concluded, or whether a navigable strait led westward into the archipelago, as both he and Barrow predicted. The immediate destination was Lancaster Sound. After crossing to Davis Strait, Parry worked slowly northward along the edge of the ice, watching eagerly for an opening across the middle pack to the Baffin shore. On July 21 he decided not to waste any more time sailing north but instead to take his ships into the ice and force a passage westward. The pack seemed impenetrable, but Parry knew from his experience the year before that the open "west water" lay on the other side, if only he could reach it. Progress was excruciatingly slow. When the ice parted slightly the ships could be towed behind their boats; usually, however, the loose chunks pressed close around the hulls and the vessels had to be warped arduously ahead. The men worked long hours with very little to show for it; during one day, for example, the warping lines were out for eleven hours but the ships made only six and a half kilometres. Parry kept at it, however, and finally, after a week in the ice, the *Hecla* and the *Griper* emerged in the "west water."

On the first day of August, Parry's two ships entered Lancaster Sound. Pushed on by a following easterly, they cruised easily down the strait. It was a remarkably open season and, as expected, the ships were not impeded by a range of mountains, or any other land barrier. They did run up against some ice, however, and Parry turned south into Prince Regent Inlet, which he explored for several days before returning to his main task, the penetration of Lancaster Sound. Keeping to the northern side of the strait Parry sailed along the shore of Devon Island and on August 22, much to his relief, passed across the mouth of a broad channel of open water leading away to the north. Now known as Wellington Channel, this passage had great significance for Parry. It indicated to him that the northern side of Lancaster Sound consisted of islands and was not a solid coastline which was going to curve across his path to join the opposite shore and halt his progress. Now the commander was convinced he was in the Northwest Passage; indeed he was convinced he had already reached the Polar Sea and would soon see Bering Strait open ahead. Continuing to the west, the expedition enjoyed favourable winds which opened a lane of water for the ships to follow.

Inevitably, of course, Parry ran out of luck, but not before the *Hecla* and *Griper* had sailed all the way to Melville Island, more than two-thirds of the way through the archipelago. Only one other arctic expedition from the Atlantic side would reach so far west in the rest of the nineteenth century.

About the middle of September the ships were halted by heavy ice off the coast of Melville Island. For several days the pack threatened to crush them against the rocky shore. Parry recognized that his first sailing season was over. Retreating to the east, he decided to pass the winter in a small bay he had noticed on the southern shore of the island. By this time the entrance was blocked by ice but the sailors managed to saw a long channel into the harbour and on September 26 the *Hecla* and *Griper* entered their winter quarters.

Parry's vessels were the first to winter so deep in the arctic archipelago and the procedures he followed to ensure a winter so far north set a precedent for other expeditions in the years ahead. There was no thought given to living on shore; the ships would be home to the men for as long as they remained locked in the ice. After the masts were taken down, decks were roofed with boards and canvas and cleared of enough equipment to provide an open space for "indoor" exercise. Once ice had formed tightly around the ships a water hole was kept constantly open in case of fire. Snow was banked against the sides to provide insulation, but as winter deepened and permanent night descended it was all the men could do to keep the temperature in their quarters much above freezing. The lower decks were heated by hot-air ducts leading from the stoves but, even so, breath commonly froze on the beams above the bedsteads.

The *Hecla* and *Griper* entered Winter Harbour at the end of September 1819 and did not sail out again until the first day of August 1820. During this time there was not a great deal for the seamen to do; boredom, and the dejection it might produce, were enemies as great as the cold. Parry waged a war on idleness which relied on precise routine and military discipline. At 5:45 each morning the men rose and immediately set to work scouring the decks of the ships with stones and sand. After breakfast at 8 A.M., the crew mustered on the quarterdeck for inspection, then did exercises while the captain inspected their quarters. Weather permitting, the sailors went ashore to walk about the harbour, a pleasant break even if the landscape was depressing in its monotony, a blank vista of ice and snow, silent as death. When weather was poor they jogged around the deck, keeping spirits up with shanties and fiddle music. At noon there was a break for lunch, after which afternoons were spent below decks picking oakum, making ropes, and repairing equipment. At six o'clock the men were inspected for a second time, then released for dinner and free time until 9 P.M., when candles were extinguished and the day ended. While the crews received a full night's sleep, officers stood regular watch and every half-hour inspected the lower decks as a precaution against fire. Every Sunday this routine was interrupted by religious services and every two weeks the thespians on board presented an evening of theatre. Crew members also were encouraged to submit prose and verse to the tiny "settlement's" weekly newspaper, the *North Georgia Gazette and Winter Chronicle.*

The men of Parry's expedition survived the winter in good health, an unusual accomplishment for the time, the result of plenty of exercise and a diet which included preserved meats and vegetables and a daily dose of lemon juice to keep off the scurvy. Whenever possible the menu was supplemented with reindeer shot on the island, but when the sun disappeared early in November so did most of the animals, leaving only the occasional fox and the wolves which prowled around the harbour "howling most piteously on the beach near us, sometimes for hours together." Only one sailor died and that was of causes unrelated to the expedition. Morale was apparently good; the only recorded instance of insubordination involved two sailors on the *Hecla* who were whipped for drunkenness. As soon as the sun reappeared in February the men went regularly to shore to gather ballast stones, hunt, and tentatively explore their island home. As spring progressed animals returned, the ground emerged in patches from beneath the snow, and pools of meltwater collected on the harbour ice. In June Parry set his men to work sawing a passage out of the bay while he crossed Melville Island with a sled party. But it was August before the ships at last were able to work free of the harbour and resume exploration in Lancaster Sound.

Struggling westward once again, Parry found the broad strait blocked by heavy masses of ice twelve to fifteen metres thick with broken hummocks piled even higher on the surface. The shifting pack forced the ships in against the coast, threatening to crush them. This was ice more awesome and unyielding than Parry had seen before. On August 8 he climbed a bluff on the coast of Melville Island and, looking southwest, saw an island on the far side of the strait which he called Bank's Land, "the most western yet discovered in the Polar Sea." But there was no way he was going to reach it. After a few more days spent waiting anxiously in sheltered coves for the ice to relent, Parry concluded there was no point continuing. As it was he needed all the luck remaining to him to manoeuvre his ships back along a coast battered by mammoth flows and into the navigable waters of eastern Lancaster Sound. Even here ice conditions frustrated hopes of exploring the Baffin shore, and the *Hecla* and *Griper* sailed away home without further discoveries.

Parry was rightly hailed as a hero on his return. He profited from an extraordinarily open navigation season to penetrate farther into the Arctic than any of his predecessors. He proved that it was possible to winter quite safely among the northern islands without being reduced by disease or frozen to death. And he had come almost within sight of the far end of a Northwest Passage, even if he had to conclude that wooden ships driven by the wind would never battle their way through the walls of ice which formed the final barrier. For all these accomplishments John Barrow considered that Parry had "opened the door to the North West Passage" and Barrow was anxious to send out another expedition to finish the job. Parry's own assessment was more modest. He remained convinced that a navigable passage existed and equally convinced that it did not lead in the direction of Melville Island. He had observed that navigation was easiest in coastal waters, where the ice tended to break up sooner in the summer and was carried off by the tides. He argued therefore that the search should be directed to the south of Lancaster Sound near the coast of North America where land explorers like Mackenzie and Hearne already reported seeing open water. For the next several decades naval expeditions into the Arctic would follow Parry's advice.

While Ross and Parry were investigating sea routes into the Arctic, the British Admiralty did not neglect the land approach. In fact the same year that Parry sailed for Lancaster Sound, 1819, another young naval lieutenant was given command of a second discovery expedition, this one to proceed overland to the Arctic coast. Like so many of his compatriots, John Franklin joined the Royal Navy when he was just a youngster, not yet fourteen years old. During the Napoleonic Wars he saw heavy action in some of the most historic sea battles, serving with Nelson at both Copenhagen and Trafalgar. After the war he was lucky enough to become involved in the arctic project. In 1818 he sailed as second in command to John Buchan on the unsuccessful venture beyond Spitsbergen. The 1819 expedition was intended to support Lieutenant Parry by proceeding to the coast and surveying it eastward of Hearne's Coppermine River, perhaps rendezvousing with Parry's ships if they were able to get that far. As it turned out, Parry made much better progress than Franklin; he was home again before the land expedition even began its coastal survey. Nonetheless Franklin's first venture into the region which would one day claim his life was noteworthy as the first successful attempt at mapping any portion of the north coast of America.

Franklin set out from home with a small party of Englishmen—naval surgeon Dr. John Richardson, Midshipmen George Back and Robert Hood, and Able-bodied Seaman John Hepburn. The rest of the expedition, which at times ballooned to fifty members, consisted of Orkney boatmen, Canadian *voyageurs*, two Inuit interpreters, and a varying number of Indian hunters, guides, and wives. After surviving a near shipwreck on the voyage out to Hudson Bay and an exhausting trip inland by canoe, York boat, and dogsled, Franklin at length reached the fur trade post of Fort Providence on Great Slave Lake at the end of July 1820.

Arrangements had been made with a North West Company trader named Wentzel that he would gather a group of Yellowknife Indians to hunt food for the expedition. With their leader, Akaitcho, or Big Foot, these natives arrived at Fort Providence to make plans. Following their advice, Franklin proceeded north up the Yellowknife River to a small lake, Winter Lake, not far from the headwaters of the Coppermine, where the men set to work building Fort Enterprise, two drafty, mud-roofed log shacks which would shelter them against the swiftly approaching frozen season. While construction was going on, Franklin intended proceeding down the Coppermine right away, but Akaitcho believed that it was too late in the year for travelling and refused to go along. Without Indian hunters to supply him, Franklin had to abandon this plan, though he did make a brief reconnaissance mission to the upper reaches of the river before settling down at Fort Enterprise for the winter.

Like Hearne before him, Franklin relied completely on the Indians to keep him supplied with food. His own men did a little fishing but for the most part they ate caribou killed by Akaitcho and his followers. This reliance became total when it was learned that several packs of supplies that were supposed to be forwarded by the fur brigades had been abandoned on the way inland. In October the migrating caribou passed the fort in vast herds; one morning Franklin estimated he saw two thousand during a brief stroll. During this time meat was stockpiled in large quantities. But as the winter progressed and animals disappeared, supplies dwindled. If food was one of Franklin's problems, cold was another. Never on his previous excursion into the Arctic had he experienced temperatures as severe as that winter. In December the daily average was –32°C; on one occasion it dropped to beyond –50°C. Outside the warming circle of the stove, living quarters were not much warmer than the out of doors; in the morning before the fire was lit it was not unusual for the temperature to be –40°C.

Dealing with the Indians called on all the diplomatic skill Franklin possessed. Gossip and rumour passed quickly among them, and Akaitcho was disturbed to hear that the fur trader at Great Slave Lake was claiming that the explorers were taking advantage of the Indians and had no intention of paying them. As well, some of Franklin's own men secretly endeavoured to turn the natives against the expedition in the hopes that it would be cancelled and they could return home safely. In the end, after testing Franklin's good faith to the limit, Akaitcho held firm and continued to provide the all-important supplies of meat.

The fort was enlivened by a love triangle involving the two midshipmen, Back and Hood. For the most part the Indians tented in the woods instead of staying at the post, but one exception was a woman who suffered from a terrible cancer which was slowly destroying her face. She wanted to remain close to Dr. Richardson and she wanted her daughter, a beautiful fifteen-year-old girl named Green Stockings, with her. According to Franklin, Green Stockings, though young, was "an object of contest between her countrymen" and already had had two husbands. Both Back and Hood wished to take her as a mistress and apparently the rivalry became so heated that seaman Hepburn had to remove the ammunition from their pistols in order to forestall a duel. Unhappily for Back, he was sent to Fort Chipewyan in October to collect supplies and Hood carried the day. The next summer Green Stockings gave birth to their daughter.

Spring was a long time coming. Early in June the explorers set out from Fort Enterprise well before the rivers and lakes were clear of ice. If they were going to accomplish anything during the summer they had to get under way, but it meant travelling under very poor conditions. Ice-covered lakes were sometimes waist-deep in meltwater, while in the partially open rivers pieces of broken ice accumulated in impassable heaps. Canoes had to be hauled on sleds, then launched across portions of open water. Finally the weary travellers reached the Coppermine and set off down it toward the Arctic Ocean.

Franklin was anxious to meet the local Inuit, who he hoped would give him useful information about the northern coast. For this reason he brought along two Inuit interpreters from Hudson Bay, Augustus and Junius. In the vicinity of Bloody Fall, where Samuel Hearne had witnessed such a horrible encounter fifty years before, these two natives made contact with a group of Inuit from the coast who were up the river fishing. These people were very skittish, especially when they learned there were Indians in the neighbourhood, and most of them ran away, but Franklin managed to talk with one old man too aged to make his escape. This was the only Inuk the explorer met during his time on the north coast. Moving on, the expedition reached the mouth of the river on July 18. Here Wentzel took his leave with a small party of *voyageurs*, promising to have the Indians stock Fort Enterprise with meat since Franklin anticipated returning there for another winter. Then the remaining twenty men embarked on their two canoes and began the exploration of the coastline toward the east.

It quickly became apparent that birchbark canoes were neither strong nor seaworthy enough to travel the Arctic coast. The small vessels were useless in high winds and heavy seas, conditions which the expedition encountered almost every day, and far too flimsy to withstand battering by the heavy pieces of ice which floated in and out with the currents. As a result, the expedition spent much of its time on shore waiting impatiently for calm weather or a favourable wind to nudge the ice out to sea. Canoes were not the only problem, of course. Game animals were scarce and before long rations were reduced to a cup of soup and a handful of pemmican each day. Almost as scarce as food was the driftwood needed to make the fires to cook it. Inevitably, with starvation looking them in the face, the men began grumbling, wanting to turn back before they got too far from their base. Finally, at Point Turnagain on the Kent Peninsula, Franklin reluctantly agreed to go no farther. Though he was disappointed at not reaching his destination, Repulse Bay, he could take consolation in the fact that his expedition had surveyed over a thousand kilometres of previously unknown shoreline. Despite the difficulties he had encountered, Franklin remained convinced that the coast was easily navigable by sailing ships and that it probably trended eastward all the way to Hudson Bay without significant barriers. In other words he believed himself to have travelled a portion of the Northwest Passage. And he was right.

But now the hard part began. Franklin and the others were about 450 km from Fort Enterprise, their winter refuge. The season was too advanced to retrace the route they had followed along the coast, where food supplies were insufficient anyway. The only alternative was to strike overland across the Barrens. The expedition embarked on August 22. Crossing the lower reaches of Bathurst Inlet, they ascended the Hood River to a point several kilometres from its mouth where a huge waterfall blocked the way. Here they paused for four days while the large, unwieldy canoes were reconstructed into a pair of smaller, lighter craft which could be carried by one man and used to ferry across lakes and rivers. The expedition was now travelling on foot, each man carrying about forty kilograms of supplies—ammunition, tools, fish nets, clothes, and blankets. Their stocks of pemmican were exhausted so they were completely dependent for food on whatever game animals, birds, and berries they could gather as they went along.

The suffering began almost immediately. Snow covered the ground and temperatures dropped well below freezing. Not far from the river they were forced to lie stormbound for two days in their tents without any food. "Our tents were completely frozen," wrote Franklin, "and the snow had drifted around them to a depth of three feet, and even in the inside there was a covering of several inches on our blankets. Our suffering from cold, in a comfortless canvas tent in such weather, with the temperature at 20° [Fahrenheit], and without fire, will easily be imagined." Yet things only got worse. Starting off again, the men were soon exhausted by the deep snow, hilly terrain, and sharp rocks which cut through their leather moccasins. Heavy winds buffeted the *voyageurs* carrying the canoes, and eventually one of the craft was smashed on the ground and abandoned. Occasionally some meat or a partridge was brought in by the hunters, but this was not enough to live on and the men subsisted on lichen boiled into a kind of stew. Often they were reduced to chewing on their old moccasins. In desperation they began to discard their packs, keeping only essentials such as guns and ammunition.

On September 26 the expedition, famished and bone weary, reached the Coppermine River about sixty-five kilometres from Fort Enterprise, only to find that they had no way to get across. The second canoe had been left behind three days before and the men were too weak to swim against the swift current. For eight days they tried and failed to ford the river, until finally one of the *voyageurs* manufactured a small canoe out of tent canvas and this carried them safely across. On the other side Franklin dispatched George Back with three of the strongest *voyageurs* to press ahead to the fort to get help from the Indians. Meanwhile the rest of the expedition picked up the march, a straggling line of ragged skeletons.

At this point, so close to their destination yet so reduced by what they had endured, the men began one by one to die. On October 6, two *voyageurs* could not continue and had to be left behind. Then Robert Hood, completely debilitated by diarrhea brought on by his diet of lichens, was too weak to go on, so Dr. Richardson and seaman Hepburn volunteered to stay with him while Franklin and the rest went on ahead. The next day four of the *voyageurs* decided they preferred to go back and wait with the Englishmen. As it turned out only one of these men, the Iroquois Michel, who had come with the expedition from Canada, arrived at the camp. Later Richardson recounted that Michel told him the other men had wandered off. There was no reason to doubt this story at first, and Richardson did not realize that during the next few days the meat that the Iroquois hunter was bringing into camp was not wolf, as he claimed, but actually pieces of the missing *voyageurs*. Either Michel had murdered them or they had died of hunger and fatigue, and he had butchered their bodies. On October 20, Michel got into an argument with Hood, now so weak he could hardly stand upright; while the others were absent, Michel shot him through the back of the head. When the other Englishmen came running, Michel claimed Hood must have shot himself. Richardson and Hepburn did not believe him, however, and now began to fear for their own lives. Without Hood to keep them back, they broke camp and set off to join Franklin at Fort Enterprise. Along the way Richardson decided that Michel was preparing another murder and so "I put an end to his life by shooting him through the head with a pistol."

When Richardson and Hepburn finally reached Fort Enterprise, they found Franklin and his remaining companions in a dreadful state. The Indians had not been able to cache any meat at the place. Back was out looking for them but meanwhile Franklin and the rest survived by burning floorboards, chewing on old leather, and eating bones boiled in water. "Upon entering the now desolate building, we had the satisfaction of embracing Captain Franklin," recalled Richardson, "but no words can convey an idea of the filth and wretchedness that met our eyes on looking around. Our own misery had stolen upon us by degrees...but the ghastly countenances, dilated eye-balls, and sepulchral voices of Mr. Franklin and those with him were more than we could at first bear." Two more *voyageurs* died of starvation before Indians finally arrived with food. As soon as they regained their strength, the survivors headed south and on December 11 they reached the safe haven of the fur trade post on Great Slave Lake. Their ordeal was over.

Franklin lost ten men on his first expedition, the worst arctic tragedy since James Knight disappeared with his entire crew in Hudson Bay in 1719. In part Franklin was the victim of bad luck; in part he was the author of his own misfortune. Franklin cannot be blamed for the fur trade rivalry, which frustrated plans to convey his supplies inland. Nor perhaps can he be blamed for not knowing how inadequate canoes would be for travelling along the northern coast. One has to question the wisdom of leading an expedition so far into the unknown with only the haziest notion how to get back again, but in the end the principal lesson to be learned was that inexperienced naval officers who took up land exploration were out of their element if they did not have constant Indian support. Unlike Hearne and Mackenzie, who were veteran fur traders, Franklin had only rudimentary knowledge of travelling and subsisting in the Canadian wilderness. During the long death march back to Fort Enterprise, he and the others proved incapable of providing for themselves from the meagre resources of the north country. Without Indian hunters and guides the expedition would never have got under way in the first place; without Indian rescuers every member surely would have perished.

Franklin eventually got back to England in the autumn of 1822, three and a half years after he had left. His fellow officer Edward Parry had not only completed the pathbreaking voyage to Melville Island during his absence, but at that very moment was testing his theory that a Northwest Passage lay close to the northern coast of the continent. Parry had sailed the previous year for Hudson Bay, where he intended resuming the exploration of its northwest corner where Captain

Middleton had broken off almost eighty years before. First of all Parry cruised up the Frozen Strait north of Southampton Island and into Repulse Bay, confirming that it was a dead end and incidentally proving the existence of the strait which had caused so much bitter controversy between Middleton and Dobbs. Parry then began a meticulous, time-consuming survey of the east coast of Melville Peninsula in search of a passage leading through it. This was the tedious, unglamorous reality of arctic exploration: the need to spend weeks, months, probing into every inlet and bay of a twisted coastline, eliminating yet another hopeless avenue of approach and adding a few more kilometres of known territory to the outline of the North, slowly emerging on the map like a photographic print gradually appearing on paper.

Parry wintered his two ships on an island near the entrance to Lyon Inlet and the next season, 1822, continued north until he arrived at the top of Foxe Basin. Here he found what he was looking for, a narrow strait running away to the west. Unfortunately it was blocked by ice and offered no passage to the ships. The expedition passed another winter nearby, but scurvy began to appear among the crews and, when the ice in the strait showed no inclination to clear out the next summer, Parry sadly returned to England.

This was a setback, not a defeat. Parry remained certain that an arctic passage existed and that it lay along the coast where Mackenzie, Hearne, and now Franklin had seen open water. The problem still to be solved was the location of the eastern entrance to the passage, and the indefatigable John Barrow was determined to have another try. "To give up the attempt before this point be tried," he urged, "would indeed be to have opened the door, at a great expense and labour, for some other nation to reap the honour and glory, and to triumph over us who have for two Centuries and a half endeavoured in vain to accomplish it."

Parry and Franklin produced book-length accounts of their adventures and were lionized by the British public. Recognized on the streets and fêted at social gatherings, they very appropriately teamed up for the next assault on the North.

Actually, Barrow conceived a three-pronged approach. Parry would take two ships through Lancaster Sound and down into Prince Regent Inlet looking for a way west. Franklin once again would travel overland, this time descending the Mackenzie River, then travelling along the coast to the west, where he would rendezvous with the naval vessel *Blossom* sent via the Pacific to Bering Strait under the command of Lieutenant F. W. Beechey.

Parry was the first to get under way, departing England in the spring of 1824. This time he was frustrated by heavy ice in Baffin Bay and for the first season he could get no farther than Port Bowen, near the north end of Prince Regent Inlet. The following summer one of his ships was wrecked and a beaten Parry left the Canadian Arctic, never to return.

Franklin left for America early in 1825 and did not even reach the northern coast until several months after Parry was forced to leave it. Travelling via New York, Upper Canada, and the old fur trade route across Lake Superior, he crossed the Northwest and descended the Mackenzie River as far as Great Bear Lake where his men built Fort Franklin, the expedition's headquarters for the winter of 1825–26. Unlike the first expedition, the second consisted overwhelmingly of British seamen, supported by a few Canadian *voyageurs* and Indian hunters. Dr. Richardson teamed up for a second time, and once again two Inuit interpreters came along, in the expectation that local Inuit would be encountered along the coast.

One important lesson that Franklin had learned on his first attempt was that canoes were not adapted to the pounding surf and heavy ice of arctic navigation. As a substitute he designed a sturdy mahogany longboat, which was able to carry over 2.5 tonnes of cargo and a crew of seven men, yet was light enough to manhandle across the interminable portages of the inland waterways. As well Franklin brought along a collapsible canvas boat, which weighed only thirty-eight kilograms and could be assembled in twenty minutes; this ingenious craft would presumably solve the problem of fording rivers on the barrens.

The winter at Fort Franklin passed without incident and on June 22, 1826, the expedition embarked in four boats for the coast. Plans called for the boats to journey together to the mouth of the Mackenzie, from where John Richardson would lead two of them to the east as far as the mouth of the Coppermine River while Franklin led the other two to the west across the top of Alaska. After separating, both parties encountered large numbers of Inuit gathered near the mouth of the river. In both cases mutual incomprehension almost led to bloodshed. Franklin's boats, grounded in a shallow bay, were surrounded by as many as three hundred natives, who attempted to pillage the craft in a very forthright, even friendly, manner. At no time did they appear to have hostile intentions, but the Inuit pressed close around the stranded sailors, carrying off supplies, trade items, even a pistol, anything that the beleaguered seamen could not preserve. Franklin gave orders not to shoot but as the looting became more intense a violent conclusion seemed likely, until suddenly the boats were released by a rising tide and the expedition scurried away down the coast. From then on Franklin kept these Inuit at bay with lowered muskets, refusing to accept their apologies or believe their protestations of friendship. Later he claimed to have heard from another group of natives that this first group was planning to murder the Englishmen, but it is very unwise to accept what one Inuit group said about another since their motives remain such a mystery.

Likewise, the modern reader cannot hope to understand what the Inuit thought about the strange intruders who arrived in their land with valuable iron goods and long sticks that burst fire. For example, John Richardson, who was similarly harassed by friendly but insistent natives as he travelled along the coast, recorded that the Inuit believed many of the British seamen were women, because in their culture it was only women who rowed the oomiaks, and they marvelled at females who had beards. Obviously, if such fundamental misunderstandings were at work, it is nearly impossible to understand why the Inuit responded as they did to the English explorers. It can, however, be observed that while the natives were rowdy and thieving they were also cheerful, friendly, and hospitable, and at no time did they make an armed attack on the boats.

After leaving the Inuit behind, Franklin continued along the coast toward his rendezvous with the *Blossom*. As on his previous trip he was frustrated by fog, storms, and ice. The north coast of Alaska is lined with low offshore islands which make navigation difficult, especially in poor visibility. Between the islands and the coast the boats would run aground and the men would have to lower themselves into the frigid water to tow them afloat. Outside the islands, however, the surf was high and the ice always threatened to pinch the boats against the land. Franklin made his way by choosing between these two dismal possibilities. By the middle of August, fearful that the boats would be wrecked and the expedition stranded, he had decided to turn back 250 km from his destination. Five days later a barge from the *Blossom*, anchored on schedule on the west coast of Alaska, managed to fight its way through the ice to Point Barrow, but when Franklin did not appear it returned to the ship and the ship sailed away. The *Blossom* returned to Alaska the next year to attempt another rendezvous. But by that time Franklin and his men had spent another winter at Great Bear Lake, Richardson having successfully completed his assignment, and were on their way home to England.

The expeditions of Parry and Franklin were remarkable achievements. They surveyed thousands of kilometres of arctic shoreline previously unknown to European mariners. Franklin charted the western end of what eventually would prove to be a navigable passage through the archipelago, and Parry drastically narrowed the area where an eastern approach to this passage might be sought. They both refined techniques for wintering in the inhospitable North. Parry pioneered the use of the dogsled, which made naval expeditions amphibious.

They did not, however, achieve their main purpose—a Northwest Passage—and Admiralty officials were understandably losing interest in the arctic project. Even John Barrow had to admit that his favourite, Parry, was beginning to repeat himself. Franklin proposed two plans for further exploration along the northern coast, but he got no response and returned to the life of a normal officer in the postwar British navy, brief periods of command followed by longer periods of unemployment. Parry was sent on one more northern expedition, a futile attempt to reach the North Pole by trekking across the ice beyond Spitsbergen. Then he left active service in favour of a series of bureaucratic positions. Meanwhile, with the Admiralty reassessing its commitment to northern exploration, private enterprise took up the challenge of the arctic project.

5

The Ordeal of
John Ross

On August 26, 1833, the whaling vessel *Isabella*, from the English port of Hull, was cruising the entrance to Lancaster Sound off the coast of Baffin Island. With twenty-seven bowhead whales already taken, the *Isabella*'s hold was two-thirds full of oil and whalebone, but the season had another month to run and Captain Humphreys had every expectation of returning home with a full vessel. The captain had just stolen a few days from whaling to make a quick search of the northern end of Prince Regent Inlet for any sign of Captain John Ross and his men of the discovery ship *Victory*, missing in the frozen north for the past four years. There was really no hope that any of the men were still alive after so long without word; but perhaps a wreck, a cairn, or some small trace of the missing expedition might be found. Humphreys and his crew saw nothing, however, and were

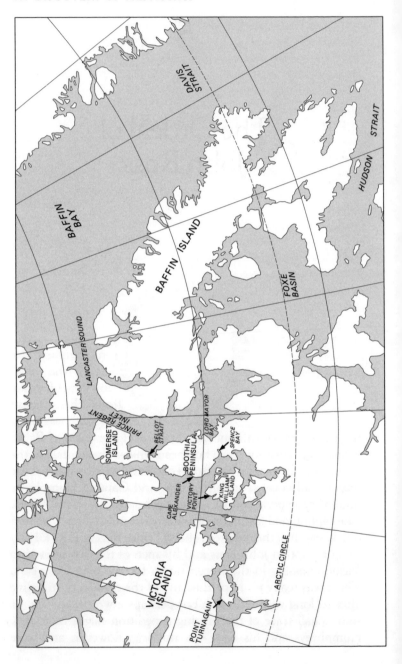

returning to the whale hunt that morning when, about eleven o'clock, the lookout spied three boats in the sound off to the southwest. There were no other ships nearby and Humphreys wondered if the boats were lost. He dispatched one of his own whaleboats to find out.

When the whaleboat drew near the strangers, the mate in command was presented with an appalling sight. Three of the castaways were so weak they lay in the bottom of the boats incapable of pulling an oar. The rest were ragged skeletons, tattered animal skins hanging loosely from their emaciated bodies, their thin faces hollow-eyed and covered with scraggly beards. Presuming such desperate-looking figures must have lost their ship, the mate asked if they were wrecked; the red-haired sailor who appeared to lead the rest answered yes. He in turn wanted to know what ship was nearby. The mate replied, "The *Isabella* of Hull, once commanded by Captain Ross" and was stunned into silence when the stranger said: "I am Captain John Ross."

"But you've been dead for two years," was all the bewildered sailor could think to answer.

Once the astonished whaler was convinced he was not seeing ghosts, he informed Ross that all of England had given him up long ago, then hurried back to his ship with the news. As Ross rowed toward the *Isabella*, a vessel he had commanded through these very waters fifteen years before, the rigging was crowded with excited whaling men, who sent up three rousing cheers to welcome the missing sailors back from the grave. Captain Ross later recalled the moment: "Unshaven since I know not when, dirty, dressed in the rags of wild beasts instead of the tatters of civilization, and starved to the very bones, our gaunt and grim looks, when contrasted with those of the well-dressed and well-fed men around us, made us all feel, I believe for the first time, what we really were, as well as what we seemed to others."

The rescued explorers were given a shave, a wash, fresh clothes, and a good meal, which they ate while telling for the first time the story of their amazing survival through four winters on the barren arctic coast. That night Ross, unused to the luxury of a comfortable bed, could only sleep sitting up in a hardbacked wooden chair.

The ordeal of the *Victory* had begun almost five years earlier, in 1828, when John Ross bought the vessel and began preparing it for an arctic expedition. Ever since his humiliating run-in with John Barrow over the existence of the Croker Mountains, Ross had been living a reluctant retirement at his castle in Scotland. His interest in the arctic project had not waned; on the contrary, he made use of his time to bone up on the new steam technology and became convinced of the value of steam power for northern navigation. Steam engines, he argued, would free sailing vessels from their dependence on capricious winds, allowing them to force their way through ice barriers and increasing their manoeuvrability among bergs and in narrow leads. Furthermore, steam allowed the use of ships of shallower draft which were better adapted to threading the open channels between ice and shore. Admittedly the new technology had drawbacks: paddlewheels were heavy and awkward, and useless in rolling seas; from a naval point of view they also had the disadvantage of interfering with firepower. Steam seemed to be a successful innovation for freshwater transportation, but the Admiralty was dead set against its introduction into the ocean-going fleet. "The introduction of Steam," declared the first lord of the Admiralty, Lord Melville, "is calculated to strike a fatal blow at the supremacy of the Empire." It was not until the invention of the screw propeller solved many of the problems associated with paddlewheels that engines began to be installed in naval vessels, in the 1840s.

When John Ross approached the Admiralty with a plan for arctic discovery, he had, then, two strikes against him—a reputation tainted by the past and an approach which smacked too much of the future. Not discouraged by an official lack of interest, the veteran explorer approached his friend Felix Booth, a wealthy gin manufacturer, who agreed to put up most of the twenty thousand pounds required to outfit the expedition. Ross found the steam yacht *Victory* making mail runs between Liverpool and the Isle of Man, and bought it; he strengthened it for arctic travel and installed new engines, designed by a leading Swedish engineer, and paddles which could be lifted out of the water to avoid collision with the ice. His preparations aroused a great deal of interest, and old arctic hands debated the pros and cons of the venture. Edward Parry, now the Admiralty hydrographer, toured the *Victory* and, while he generously stated that Ross "has a better chance of succeeding than any of us," he also warned that "there is, in the whole thing, rather too much that is new and untried; and this is certainly not the kind of service on which novelties of that sort ought first to be tried." Nevertheless, Parry concluded, "it is a bold, public-spirited undertaking."

Parry's warning about untried novelties turned out to be only too accurate. The *Victory* left home in May 1829, and almost immediately the machinery began misbehaving. The boilers leaked so badly that pumps had to be kept going constantly to bail the ship. Even when they were caulked with a strange mixture of dung and potatoes, the boilers continued to leak. The engines themselves broke down repeatedly. Without replacement parts, repairs had to be carried out using pieces manufactured out of whatever materials were at hand. When they were functioning, the engines moved the vessel at a top speed of only five kilometres per hour, and then for only hours at a time before some new part failed, "as if it had been predetermined," wrote Ross, "that not a single atom of all this machinery should be aught but a source of vexation, obstruction and evil."

Ross had purchased a whaling vessel, the *John*, to accompany the expedition as a supply ship. It was his intention that, after leaving its supplies, the *John* would salvage whatever remained of the wreck of the *Fury*, the ship lost by Parry in Prince Regent Inlet four years before, then spend a summer whaling in Davis Strait before returning to England with a cargo of oil and baleen to offset the cost of the expedition. However, the vessels had not even left British waters before the crew of the whaler refused to go any farther without a guarantee from Ross that they would receive at least a minimum wage. The commander did not agree, the mutineers jumped ship, and the *Victory* proceeded without its consort.

Putting these delays and disappointments behind him, Ross crossed the Atlantic, rounding Greenland into Davis Strait early in July. Although the engines continued to perform badly, weather and ice conditions now favoured the expedition and the ship crossed Baffin Bay to Lancaster Sound without any trouble. Ross planned to follow Edward Parry's suggestion that a passage along the northern coast of North America must lead out of the bottom of Prince Regent Inlet. Parry had been frustrated in his attempts to locate this passage; Ross hoped not only to find it but to sail through it to the open coastal waters to the west, already explored by John Franklin.

By August 11 the *Victory* was cruising down the inlet close under the bold shores of Somerset Island. "The more we saw of this coast," remarked Ross, "the higher the cliffs were found; while in some places projecting into horizontal shelves, and at others putting on an aspect of walls, castles and turrets, with shapes even more fantastical..." The *Fury* had been abandoned in a small bay on the Somerset coast, and Ross was relieved to find the stores Parry had piled on the beach still intact, though there was no sign of the disabled wreck itself. After salvaging two years' worth of canned meat and vegetables, cocoa, sugar, and flour, the expedition continued down the inlet, entering a region of the Arctic never before visited by European ships. Ice kept the *Victory* three or four kilometres out from shore so that a meticulous survey was impossible. As a result, Ross did not locate Bellot Strait, a narrow passage which divides Somerset Island from Boothia Peninsula and the American mainland. Mistaking the entrance to this strait for a bay, Ross missed the opportunity to proceed westward, instead sailing into what proved to be a virtual *cul de sac* from which he almost did not return.

The end of September found the *Victory* trapped in the ice in Lord Mayor Bay on the southeast coast of Boothia, not far from the isthmus which joins the peninsula to the mainland. The weather was cold and snowy, the ice was pressing up against the coast, and Ross realized that this was as far as he was going to get until the next summer. He began the usual preparations for wintering in the North: decks were roofed over with canvas and boards, snow was banked against the hull, stoves were located to keep the crew's quarters at a livable temperature. One of the first chores was to rid the ship of its worthless steam engines. Most of the machinery was dismantled and cast onto the beach, where pieces were found over one hundred years later. "There was not one of us who did not hail this event with pleasure," Ross recalled. "The enemy was at last at our feet."

Like Parry, Ross knew the virtues of a rigid schedule. Even though there was little for them to do, the men were roused every morning at 6 A.M. and set to work scrubbing the lower decks with hot sand for two hours. After breakfast, mornings were occupied with work around the ship until the noon meal. In the afternoon, weather permitting, work continued out of doors onshore; otherwise the men took compulsory exercise on the upper deck. A healthy tea was served at five. In the evening most of the sailors attended night school, where they learned reading, writing, arithmetic, and basic navigation. At 10 P.M. hammocks were slung and, aside from the night watch, the ship fell quiet for another day.

Early in January 1830, Ross made initial contact with a band of Inuit who were living in a small village of snowhouses not far away. These were the Netsilik people, who inhabited the central Arctic in the vicinity of King William Island and Boothia and spent the winter hunting seal through the sea ice. Friendly relations were soon established between Europeans and natives and continued all winter. The Inuit were pleased to receive iron goods from the strangers in return for skin clothing, snowshoes, sled dogs, seal meat, and fresh fish. The Inuit were also amusing and novel companions; visiting back and forth between the ship and their houses helped to break the monotony of a long winter trapped in the ice. But perhaps most importantly, the natives provided Ross with detailed information about the lie of the land, helping him to plan his spring sledding expeditions and going along as guides and hunters.

Basically the problem Ross had set himself was to forge a link between his winter harbour and Point Turnagain, the point at which John Franklin had turned back during his visit to the coast in 1821. Between these two locations lay about nine hundred kilometres of unexplored coastline. In order to reach that coast Ross had to find a way around Boothia, perhaps via a passage to the south, perhaps back toward the north, he did not know. He planned to find out by dispatching dogsled expeditions in the early spring.

Parry had initiated the use of sleds, or sledges as they are often called, but it was Ross and his nephew James who were the first naval explorers to use this piece of native technology to great effect. The sledging season lasted from April to June. Before that time the sun was continuously below the horizon and temperatures were too severe for prolonged travel; later the snow was getting soggy, ice was covered with meltwater, and streams were beginning to open. During the spring of 1830 the Rosses, with their native guides, made five trips. On one of these James satisfied himself that no sea passage ran to the west beneath Boothia. Next he went on a twenty-eight-day excursion across the isthmus to Spence Bay, then across a frozen strait to the tip of King William Island. James Ross knew how difficult it was to draw conclusions about the nature of a landscape buried under ice and snow.

> The question with me was, whether we were in reality skirting a continent, or whether all this irregular land might not be a chain of islands. Those unacquainted with frozen climates like the present, must recollect that when all is ice, and all one dazzling mass of white; when the surface of the sea itself is tossed up and fixed into rocks, while the land is on the contrary, very often flat, if not level; when, in short, there is neither water nor land to be seen...it is not always so easy a problem as it might seem on a superficial view, to determine a fact which appears, in words to be extremely simple.

Ross, however, did conclude that he was following the mainland; he called it King William's Land. He was able to get as far as Victory Point on the northwest coast before a dwindling stock of provisions forced him to turn back, convinced that he was just a few days short of Point Turnagain. He was not, of course, but it would be another eight years before the true configuration of the coast was discovered.

John Ross intended to sail in search of a way around Boothia to the west as soon as summer would release the *Victory* from its icy prison. But release did not come. The ice held firm and the ship was able to move only a few kilometres before it was caught for another winter. "Some of us could not help calculating the number of centuries it would require to make a single north-west passage, at this rate," the commander remarked wryly.

The dark season passed slowly. Impatient and bored, Ross and his men fought off a black depression which threatened their well-being every bit as much as the cold and snow. "Amid all its brilliancy, this land, the land of ice and snow, has ever been, and ever will be a dull, dreary, heart-sinking, monotonous waste," he complained, "under the influence of which the very mind is paralyzed, ceasing to care or think...for it is but the view of uniformity and silence and death." Ross observed the Inuit, who seemed so cheerfully adapted to the northern environment, and recognized frankly that his discomfort was psychological as well as physical. "We were here out of our element, as much in the philosophy of life as in the geography of it."

At length spring returned and the sledges were broken out for another short season of overland exploration. The highlight of the year's travels was the location of the magnetic north pole. Observations had already pinpointed the general area where it would be found; on June 1, 1831, at eight o'clock in the morning, James Ross arrived at the spot at Cape Adelaide on the west coast of Boothia. "I believe I must leave it to others to imagine the elation of mind with which we found ourselves now at length arrived at this great object of our ambition," he wrote. "It almost seemed as if we had accomplished every thing that we had come so far to see and to do; as if our voyage and all its labours were at an end, and that nothing now remained for us but to return home and be happy for the rest of our days."

But there would be no return home, at least not yet. Once again, that summer the ship could make no headway against ice and storm, managing to progress just 6.5 km before seeking shelter in yet another coastal harbour. Ross indulged his frustration by railing against the relentless ice which would not let him go. "To us, the sight of ice was a plague, a vexation, a torment, an evil, a matter of despair." The days resumed their depressing regularity. There were no Inuit visitors this winter to relieve the tedium; even catching a mouse was an incident marked with great interest. Added to the boredom was a growing anxiety about the future. It appeared possible that the *Victory* might never break free of the ice. Provisions would not last indefinitely. The sailors, cut off from their natural element, the sea, seemed trapped in a frozen waste-land.

Captain Ross decided that the expedition's only hope for survival was to abandon the *Victory* and strike out overland. The plan was to mount the boats on sled runners, along with whatever provisions remained, and haul them north along the shore of Prince Regent Inlet as far as the site of the *Fury* wreck, where more supplies and three extra boats were cached. There the ice would perhaps be open enough to launch the boats and the expedition could make its way out into Lancaster Sound where it could probably hail a passing whaler. During the spring of 1832 the crew laboured tirelessly, hauling boat-loads of provisions up the coast to establish depots for the long trek which was to come. It was arduous work, performed in temperatures well below freezing. The ice surface out from the shore was broken and hummocky, so work parties followed a relatively smooth ledge of ice attached to the coastline. This made the travelling easier but it meant tracing all the ins and outs of an irregular shore. One cache, for instance, was only 13 km north of the ship, yet the men had to trek 175 km to supply it. Finally, on May 29, the string of depots leading to the north was complete and the expedition bid farewell to the *Victory* for the last time.

Ross's careful preparations paid dividends. The boats had to be left along the way—they proved too bulky to handle over the rough ice—but after a month's hike all the crewmen straggled into the camp on Somerset Island, exhausted and snowblind, but alive. There was no open water in the inlet, so Ross set his men to work building a shelter. Somerset House, as he called it, was a frame structure, 9.5 m long and almost 5 m wide, covered with canvas sails. One-half was divided into cabins for the officers; the other side was a large room for the sailors. Here the anxious explorers lived, waiting for a chance to escape. On August 1, that chance came: a channel of water opened along the coast. Quickly loading three boats with enough provisions to last two months, the men embarked, eight to a boat. Yet almost as suddenly as the ice had opened it closed again, forcing the boats ashore about thirteen kilometres from Fury beach. For several days they camped at the foot of a cliff, while rocks dislodged by the gradual thaw rained down on them. Even though it was August, snow covered the ground and temperatures at night were below zero. On September 3, the party reached the top of Somerset Island; anxious watch was kept but day after day, for three weeks, the ice formed one impenetrable barrier out in the sound from coast to coast. Finally Ross gave up and ordered his men back to Fury beach and a fourth winter trapped in the Arctic.

Somerset House proved a comfortable enough home once it had been insulated with a thick wall of snow and heated with a pair of stoves, but spirits were drooping badly. For three years a diet of canned foods and lemon juice had kept the men remarkably fit; now their health began to deteriorate. To make matters worse, the weather was particularly foul for much of the winter, confining all hands to the house and making regular exercise impossible. In February 1833, the carpenter, who had been sick for some time, died of scurvy. Before the month ended two others showed signs of sharing the same fate. All in all it was a sickly, dejected group of men who prepared the boats that spring for yet another attempt to escape the Arctic's frozen grip, conscious that this was probably their last chance.

It was the middle of August before the three boats could get under way, but finally Ross and his crew were blessed with an open season. Making good time under sail and by oar, the small craft emerged from Prince Regent Inlet and made their way along the top of Baffin Island, seeking the whaling fleet which soon would leave the area for home. On August 26, camped on shore, the men spotted a sail out in the sound. They hurriedly launched the boats and rowed frantically toward the ship, only to have it sail out of sight. However, another vessel soon came into view, the *Isabella* of Hull, and the Ross expedition was rescued from its four-year imprisonment in the Canadian North.

Like a conquering hero, Ross was welcomed back from the grave with honours and celebration. Understandably he felt that his reputation as an arctic traveller was vindicated. He had succeeded, where Edward Parry had failed, in penetrating Prince Regent Inlet; men under his command had explored an unknown stretch of coast and made important scientific discoveries; and he had managed to bring almost his entire crew back alive after spending longer in the North than any other European explorer.

However, the old commander was never far from controversy. The expedition had lasted so much longer than anyone had expected he had no money to pay his crew's wages. Responding to a wave of popular sympathy for what the expedition had endured and accomplished, the Admiralty agreed to underwrite the outstanding wages and the next spring Parliament voted to reimburse Felix Booth for his investment and grant Ross himself £5000. The captain gave £250 to his nephew James but relations between the kinsmen were strained by jealousy. James wanted more credit for his undeniable contributions to the expedition; John was a little reluctant to give it, perhaps fearing that the younger man was pushing him out of the spotlight. John Ross began to see conspiracies linking James with his old nemesis, John Barrow, who still delighted in reminding the public at every opportunity about the "Croker Mountains." "He now stands openly forward, leaguing with my bitter antagonist to attach discredit to my name," ranted the commander about his nephew. "He strikes when he ought to protect; he calumniates when he ought to vindicate." Despite such angry accusations, the two managed to settle their differences. James went on to gain great fame in his own right as an explorer of the Antarctic; John continued an active life as a diplomat and even managed to make one more voyage to the Arctic, at the age of seventy-three, before his death in 1856.

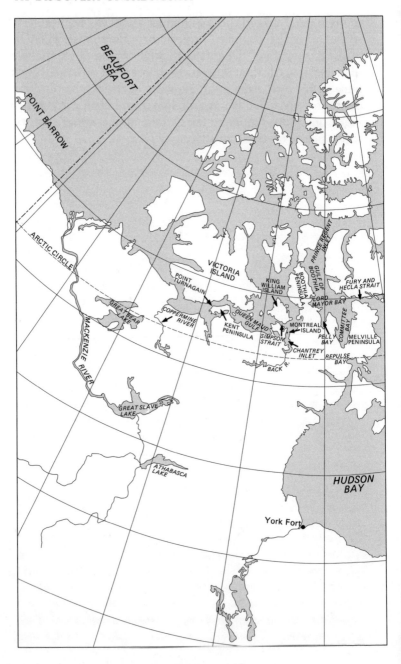

6

Completing
the Coastline

The Hudson's Bay Company blew hot and cold on the subject of arctic exploration. Ever since Arthur Dobbs had stirred up so much trouble with his criticisms of the company, officials recognized that it was politic to appear interested in the project, or at least not to seem positively opposed to it. But for many years there was no good reason for the Honourable Company to be much interested in northern exploration. The Arctic was distant and almost completely unknown. From what traders in the bay did know, it offered few prospects of profitable returns, either in furs or any other product. A Northwest Passage might only cause problems for the company, opening a vast new territory to competing merchants. The enterprising march of Samuel Hearne in the 1770s did little to contradict this assessment of the North, and the company pretty much left arctic exploration to others, always willing to cooperate but not mounting expeditions of its own. It was, after all, a trading company, not an explorers' club.

After union with the North West Company in 1821, however, the Hudson's Bay Company began to take a more direct interest in the arctic project. The fur trade was moving inexorably northward and would soon be brought to the shores of the Arctic Ocean. Russian traders belonging to the Russian American Company were reportedly moving into the area from their headquarters at Kodiak Island off the south coast of Alaska. These Russian rivals had territorial ambitions on the Pacific Coast and it was now in the Hudson's Bay Company's best interests to try to outflank them in the North. Furthermore, since the company relied on the goodwill of the British government for the periodic renewal of its trading privileges, it could not overlook any opportunity to curry official favour.

The Hudson's Bay Company was most effective when it came to exploration by land. Its knowledge of arctic sailing was limited to the annual supply voyage through Hudson Strait; the Admiralty was much better informed in exploring arctic waters. On land, however, the company was in its element, able to draw on a corps of seasoned inland travellers and over a century of hard-won experience. During John Franklin's second overland expedition to the Arctic shore, 1825–27, the company was content to play second fiddle, freighting supplies, offering the hospitality of its posts, and lending servants to the expedition.

This cooperation continued into the next decade when a rescue effort was mounted to go in search of John Ross and the *Victory*, missing in Prince Regent Inlet for three winters. The rescue expedition was led by naval officer George Back, a veteran of both Franklin excursions. It assembled at the eastern end of Great Slave Lake in the fall of 1833 with the intention of following a river that, the Indians said, drained the Barrens south and east to the Arctic Ocean. Before he set off in the spring of 1834, Back was informed that Ross had returned safely to England, so his objective became the continuation of the survey of the arctic coastline. Descending the wild river, now known as the Back, in an unwieldy boat heavily laden with foodstuffs and a crew of ten, the expedition reached the coast at the head of Chantrey Inlet on the western flank of Boothia Peninsula. Back intended taking the boat westward toward Point Turnagain, Franklin's point of farthest advance in 1821, but the expedition got no farther than the top of the deep inlet before heavy ice halted its progress. Back and his companions returned to Great Slave Lake without settling any of the questions still asked about the complicated stretch of coastline between Point Turnagain and Hudson Bay.

The Hudson's Bay Company supported Back with food, canoes, and men free of charge, but privately its traders admitted an intense dislike for the explorer. He was, apparently, a vain and over-bearing man, mistrusted for his easy manner with the natives and resented for his impertinence, a relative newcomer to the country masquerading as an old hand. "He descends the river through the Barren Lands in dreadful weather," observed one company man caustically, "but is never too wet, cold or exhausted to forget to sprinkle the names of his most distinguished patrons over the most forbidding landscape in all America." Another trader spoke for many of his colleagues: "George Back is the theme of all their aversion and contempt."

Back had taken with him on the expedition a young surgeon named Richard King. King developed decided opinions about the methods and direction of future arctic ventures and, returning to England, attempted to gain support for an expedition of his own. However sensible his views on the North, King expressed them intemperately and managed to alienate all possible patrons. Hudson's Bay Company officials took a dislike to him for his forthright criticisms of the fur trade's impact on the native people. Governor George Simpson was much disturbed at the thought of such a man leading another overland party through his territory, asking favours, then penning scurrilous attacks on the trade. The time seemed to be right for the Hudson's Bay Company to stop playing a supporting role to various upstart naval officers and take on the part of leading actor.

In the early summer of 1836, Governor Simpson commissioned an expedition to complete the survey of the Arctic coast, the first initiative taken by the company in this direction in fifty years. As leader he appointed Peter Warren Dease, a fifty-year-old chief trader who had lived for many years in the Athabasca and Mackenzie River districts. Dease had given valuable assistance to John Franklin's second expedition, procuring food for the explorers and overseeing the construction of their winter base on Great Bear Lake. An experienced and able northern traveller, he was a natural choice to command the new venture. Along with Dease, the governor sent his young cousin, Thomas Simpson, as scientist-surveyor and second in command. Educated in Scotland as a clergyman, Thomas was fresh out of university and without a position when his kinsman George offered him a job. Thomas accepted and spent the next seven years in the fur country. But instead of the exciting, romantic life he had expected when he left home, his work had been clerical and dull. "It shall go very hard with me if I ever turn copyist again," he remarked when he was at length liberated from this drudgery; "seven years of that work well nigh made a fool of me." Finally his desire for more active duty was satisfied and in the winter of 1836–37 he trekked overland from Red River to join his partner, Dease, at Athabasca Lake.

The objective of the expedition was to complete the survey of the Arctic coastline begun by John Franklin. This had more than academic interest. It was presumed that the shore was fringed by a channel of open water during the summer months so that the discovery of the coast would also be the discovery of the Northwest Passage. During the open season of 1837, the two explorers came down the Mackenzie River with a party of fourteen men in two open boats and rowed away to the west, intending to reach Point Barrow, a feat Franklin had failed to accomplish. They made their way in thick fog and squally weather through a narrow channel of water between the beach and the sea ice. When the breeze blew from the north, the ice came down against the land, blocking the way forward; an offshore wind moved the floes away from the coast and the boats could make headway. Finally, late in July, the expedition was beset for good; the ice showed no sign of relenting. Franklin had had the same experience and had turned back. This time Simpson and Dease had a few days to spare before the prospect of winter would force them to retreat. Leaving Dease with the boats, Simpson and five others proceeded on foot, taking along a canvas canoe to carry them across river mouths and inlets. Not far from Point Barrow they came to an Inuit camp, where they borrowed an oomiak to resume the trip by water. Early on the morning of the fourth day, Simpson and his men reached the point; the entire length of the north coast of what is now Alaska had been travelled for the first time.

Simpson and Dease encountered Inuit all along the coast. Aside from the good-natured pilfering so often experienced by explorers, the native people were friendly and helpful. Yet Simpson, whose account of the expedition was the only one published, was very suspicious of them. He called their friend-liness "deceitful good-humour" and advised that it was better to intimidate them with a determined display of arms than to court them with offers of friendship. When the Inuit got guns, he warned darkly, it would not be safe for Europeans to travel in the Arctic. Simpson did not confine his prejudice to the Inuit. He had very little good to say about the Chipewyan either, finding them intemperate, wasteful, and lazy. And his opinion of mixed bloods, formed during his residence at Red River, was that they were "roving and indolent" with "uncon-trollable passions," frivolous and given to violence. Such arrogant disregard for native cultures was unusual among fur traders, who for the most part admired the natives' wilderness skills and had a keen sense of the degree to which the trade relied on Indian goodwill. Thomas Simpson's contempt for native people led directly to his mysterious death a few years later.

But first the expedition had much to accomplish. Returning along the coast to the Mackenzie River, the men ascended the river to Great Bear Lake where, at the eastern end, an advance party had begun construction of a residence. By the onset of winter a cluster of three small log houses was completed and dignified with the name Fort Confidence. With Indian hunters supplying food, the explorers waited out an especially severe winter, enduring temperatures of more than sixty degrees below zero. For six months the mercury did not rise above freezing. On occasion the men huddled at night with their sled dogs for warmth, but so cold was it that several of the animals froze to death. "Our winter fare consists of caribou and musk-ox meat, whitefish and an occasional trout," Simpson wrote his brother Alexander. "We were threatened with starvation at the outset; but by dint of dispensing all hands we got over that and now enjoy abundance."

Simpson had been disappointed at the outset at having to share leadership of the expedition. His morbid frustration at being denied the sole glory of the expedition's accomplishments deepened during the winter. An egotistical man, he was prone to depression when his ambitions were thwarted, his talents unrewarded. Governor Simpson knew his cousin's instability, which was one reason why Dease had been put in charge of the expedition to organize the mundane but all-important details, which his mercurial assistant would have been prone to overlook. The younger explorer, however, conceded nothing to his partner. "I, and I alone, have the well-earned honour of uniting the Arctic to the great Western Ocean, and of unfurling the British flag on Point Barrow," he wrote his brother. As far as Simpson was concerned, the older man was an actual hindrance; he dismissed his efforts with condescension. "Dease is a worthy, indolent, illiterate soul and moves just as I give the impulse."

With the return of warmer weather Simpson's mood apparently improved, and early in June the expedition left Fort Confidence to cross overland to the upper Coppermine River. After a hair-raising run down this river, swollen with spring run-off, the explorers reached the Arctic coast and turned their boats to the east. For many kilometres they followed in the track of John Franklin, but this did not make the going any easier. Simpson described how the men worked the boats through heavy ice:

Often, when the ice was not quite firm enough to make portages with safety, we hauled the boats upon it; and, holding on by the gunwales, all hands continued jumping and pressing down till it began to yield; and, the boats sinking into the water, we scrambled on board, and by main force pushed aside the pieces thus separated. At other times, one party was stationed upon the rocks, with iron-shod poles, to shove against the ice; another upon the ice, to shove against the rocks; and, when an opening the breadth of the boats could be thus formed, the remaining hands passed them through, one at a time: those with the poles holding on with all their might, lest the ice should close, like a pair of nut-crackers and deprive us of the means of either advancing or retreating.

Ice and weather conditions combined to slow the expedition to a crawl and ultimately, on August 9, to stop it altogether just short of Point Turnagain. There was not a patch of open water visible from camp and a succession of wintry gales swept the rocky shore. Once again Simpson elected to continue on foot. With a party of seven men, he trekked across the top of the Kent Peninsula to its eastern end, Cape Alexander, where the sea suddenly opened into a broad, ice-free gulf. With provisions running low, Simpson had to return to the boats but what he had seen made him confident a navigable passage existed along the coast. One more season's exploration would tell the tale.

Re-embarking in their boats, Simpson, Dease, and the others hurried back along the coast before they were trapped by swiftly approaching winter. On September 3, they entered the Coppermine. In June the river had been in flood; in September water was low, filled with rocks and rapids. Boats had to be tracked against the heavy current, the men spilling onto the shore to haul on ropes. "The strain on the lines was often so great, that the trackers, even on all fours, could scarcely maintain their ground," recalled Simpson. The men struggled along the river banks, waist-high in frigid water or cutting their feet and bruising their legs on the sharp rocks. It was painful, back-breaking toil for several days until they reached a spot above the rapids where the boats were cached for the winter. Finishing the journey on foot, they arrived back at Fort Confidence on September 14.

The winter of 1838–39, their second at Great Bear Lake, passed uneventfully for the explorers. Simpson seems not to have desponded at the fact that he had not completed a survey of the coast, perhaps because he was so confident of doing so the next summer. He did cast aside all reticence about criticizing Dease, writing to Governor Simpson that his partner "is disposed to risk nothing; and is, therefore, the last man in the world for a discoverer. I write not in anger but in sorrow; I esteem Mr. Dease for his upright private character, while I cannot help regarding him and his followers as a dead weight upon the expedition." But the governor was not disposed to credit Thomas's complaint; caution, after all, was the trait which had commended Dease in the first place. If Thomas hoped to be given sole command of next season's exploration, he was disappointed; Dease would stay.

The season of 1839 was a completely different story from the previous year. A mild spring allowed the expedition to start down the coast two weeks earlier, and open ice conditions favoured a speedy passage. As a result, the boat reached Point Turnagain almost a month sooner. Pressing on, the explorers cruised the south shore of Queen Maud Gulf and then were surprised to discover a passage, named Simpson Strait, which showed that King William Island was just that, an island, not part of the mainland as James Ross had supposed. In the middle of August they reached a cache left by George Back on Montreal Island in Chantrey Inlet. The objective of the expedition was attained: the discoveries of Franklin were joined to those of Back. Sixty-seven years after the first European, Samuel Hearne, reached the Arctic coast, its tortuous complexities were revealed at last for the mapmakers of the world.

There remained one final unknown, Boothia. Was it a long peninsula and therefore a barrier to navigation on the coast, or was it an island, divided from the mainland of America by a navigable strait? Simpson and Dease, elated at their success, determined to find out. With a week left to pursue their voyage eastward, the two explorers started up the western side of Boothia, looking for the passage they hoped existed. However, before they could come to any definite conclusions, they were forced by the lateness of the season to turn back. Late in September they arrived at Fort Confidence after what Simpson truthfully called "by far the longest voyage ever performed in boats on the Polar Sea." Rather than endure another winter at the fort, they travelled overland to the Mackenzie, up the river to Great Slave Lake, and out of the country.

Simpson returned to the south full of plans for a final journey to the Arctic. "All that now remains unknown of Arctic America is the great gulph of Boothia (otherwise Prince Regent's Inlet), from whence we returned; and none shall take it out of my hands," he wrote to a friend. Hoping to get under way in the summer of 1840, Simpson presented his plan to the Hudson's Bay Company, but his ambitions were temporarily dashed when his uncle suggested that instead of going north again he take a year's leave of absence. Dease was going on leave and apparently the governor did not trust his nephew to go alone. Thomas was deeply disappointed. He was too impatient to wait another year and did not want Dease along anyway. "Fame I will have but it must be alone," he candidly declared to his uncle. At Red River he waited irritably to learn if company officials in London would over-rule the governor and permit him to go. As the weeks passed and no word came, Simpson fell once again into a sullen depression. "I never remember being thoroughly in the blues in my life before—a melancholy reward certainly for all I have done and suffered of late!" His feelings were hurt, his talents ignored, his ambition apparently baffled.

On June 3, in London, a letter was signed by the governing committee of the Hudson's Bay Company authorizing Simpson to proceed immediately on an expedition of discovery to the Arctic coast. The young explorer never read it. In Red River he had grown so exasperated at the silence that seemed to greet his plans he decided to go to England to present his case in person. On June 6, he left the settlement on horseback with two mixed-blood acquaintances to travel east via the United States. Overtaking a larger party, Simpson joined it for a few days but finding the pace too slow travelled on ahead with his original companions and two other mixed bloods. According to the testimony of the latter, on the evening of June 14, as the small party made camp, Simpson shot to death the two men with whom he had left Red River, explaining to the others that the victims would have murdered him if he had not acted first. The two survivors raced back with the news to the larger caravan, which immediately proceeded ahead to investigate. As the riders approached Simpson's camp, a single shot was heard and Simpson was found lying dead with his gun in his hand and his head blown away.

The verdict of an investigation into this affair was that Simpson for some reason shot his two companions, then took his own life. His views on mixed bloods were, after all, well known. During his residence at Red River earlier in the decade, he had engaged in an infamous set-to with one of the mixed-blood residents and as lately as the previous January he had written to a friend, "I have not the least sympathy with the depraved and worthless half breed population." There were questions raised about the incident, chiefly by Thomas's brother Alexander, who was inclined to believe that Thomas was the victim of vengeful mixed bloods who thought he was carrying the secret to the Northwest Passage and intended stealing it from him. He shot his victims in self-defence, argued Alexander, and was either mortally wounded by them or was murdered by the others when they came upon him. However, Alexander presented no compelling evidence to prove his theory. Given Simpson's contempt for native people and his gloomy, frustrated state of mind, it is quite possible to imagine him allowing some slight difference of opinion to escalate into violence. But to this day the exact cause of Simpson's death remains an unsolved mystery.

Thomas Simpson was egotistical, self-pitying, bigoted, and unstable; he was also a daring and resourceful northern traveller. The Hudson's Bay Company did not have many like him. For several years plans to discover the true outline of Boothia, what George Simpson called "the final problem in the Geography of the northern hemisphere," languished. Then, in 1844, a worthy successor appeared.

John Rae was an Orkneyman, bred to the sea and educated as a doctor. He joined the Hudson's Bay Company in 1833 as a ship's surgeon but spent most of the next decade in the vicinity of Moose Fort in James Bay. Rae distinguished himself by his ability to travel rapidly across great distances in the worst weather, usually on foot. Once he hiked non-stop on snow-shoes from Red River to Sault Ste. Marie, managing to gain a kilogram of weight in the process. He was "very muscular and active, full of animal spirits," remarked a fellow trader, "one of the best snow-shoe walkers in the service." The governor, who prided himself on his own ability to get around the fur country in record time, was struck by Rae's strength and perseverance and nominated him for the arctic venture. "As regards the management of the people and endurance of toil, either in walking, boating or starving, I think you are better adapted for this work than most of the gentn. with whom I am acquainted in the country."

Thomas Simpson's original plan had called for a party to go down the Back River, then follow the coastline eastward until it reached Hudson Bay. John Rae turned this plan around. He decided to approach the Arctic from the bay side, making Repulse Bay his point of departure and the Back his line of retreat. However, Rae agreed with Simpson that a small party travelling light and fast was best. He took eleven men and only four months' worth of food, intending to depend for the rest on his rifle and his fish nets. He delayed departure for a year while he learned some rudimentary navigational skills, then the Rae expedition departed York Factory for the north in June 1846, aboard two open boats, the *Magnet* and the *North Pole*. Rae kept his instructions from the governor stuffed inside his luggage where they would not get wet. "The eyes of all, who take an interest in the subject, are fixed on the Hudsons

Bay Company; from us the world expects the final settlement of the question that has occupied the attention of our country for two hundred years...."

After a six-week voyage up the west coast of Hudson Bay, Rae and his party arrived at the head of Repulse Bay toward the end of July, leaving themselves another month at least for exploring. Four Inuit were on the shore of the bay when Rae arrived. They drew him a rough map which indicated that only a narrow isthmus of land divided Repulse from water on the other side, and most of the strip was apparently occupied by lakes. This news dashed one of Governor Simpson's fondest hopes, that a passage of water divided Melville Peninsula from the mainland, but it indicated to Rae that he might get a boat across the isthmus without much difficulty. These were sturdy, clinker-built craft, almost seven metres long, designed especially for northern service. As it turned out, it was not as easy to manhandle one of them across the land bridge as Rae expected. Streams were shallow and rock-filled; the men had to track the boat along much of the route and carry it over several portages. On the lakes, poles propelled it forward when there was no favouring breeze to fill the knockdown sails. These bodies of water had tortuous shorelines, which made it very difficult to locate the waterways leading out of them.

It took eight days to make the sixty-kilometre crossing. When they reached the other side at Committee Bay, the deep southern arm of the Gulf of Boothia, the ice was so thick they could advance only a short distance before having to give it up as a lost cause. Leaving the boat in the care of four of his men, Rae walked back to Repulse where he found the rest of his party hard up for food, barely managing to keep themselves going on fish and a bit of caribou meat. Obviously, if the expedition was going to survive a winter in this spot, and Rae intended to try, preparations would have to be made. Given ice conditions in Committee Bay, it seemed unlikely any more progress could be made with the survey that season. Rae sent six men back across the isthmus to collect the boat and began to consider the erection of a proper habitation.

Rae was proposing to do something never before voluntarily

attempted by any other explorer: wintering above the treeline without a ship in which to live. Using the materials at hand, he and his men set to work constructing a shelter out of stones. When it was finished, and appropriately christened Fort Hope, it measured 6 m long by 4.2 m deep, with a roof of animal skins and canvas supported on oars and masts from the boats. The door was a flap of caribou hide; the walls were more than half a metre thick. The commander slept in his own cramped quarters behind a canvas drop sheet. The others, Orkneymen, mixed bloods, French Canadians, Indian, and Inuit, lived together in the larger room, huddled for warmth around a stone fireplace. The atmosphere inside was thick with tobacco smoke and the stench of unwashed men. The chimney, badly constructed, did not draw properly unless the door was open, an inconvenience which meant that in the dead of winter the temperature inside Fort Hope was often twenty degrees below zero.

After the house was finished, food was the next preoccupation. Repulse Bay turned out to be well situated for wintering. It was located not far from the path of migrating caribou herds, and salmon were plentiful in the coastal waters. In all, the men killed 162 caribou and 200 partridges for the winter. Seals provided oil for lamps and, in the absence of wood, moss and other plant life served as fuel for the fire. The men were hardly comfortable, but they survived.

As fall deepened into winter, the days followed a fairly set routine. Breakfast was the first of two daily meals. "This meal usually consisted of boiled venison," reported Rae, "the water with which it was cooked being converted into a very excellent soup by the addition of some deer's blood, and a handful or two of flour." The evening meal was identical. Regular chores involved hunting, fishing, and gathering fuel. Several small outbuildings served as storehouses; these were joined by tunnels under the snow. Occasionally the local Inuit paid a visit, which helped to break the monotony. Evenings were spent wrapped in skin blankets smoking and talking in the stone house, invariably left dark and cold by the need to conserve fuel. When the weather allowed, the men played football outside. After a storm, snow had to be shovelled away from the door of the house and pathways re-established. On one occasion it took two days of steady digging to find one of the boats, buried under more than two metres of drifted snow. On January 8, 1847, the lowest temperature of the winter was recorded, -44°C. Later, rations were reduced to a single meal a day. As fuel ran low it had to be kept for cooking, and there was even less for heating the house. The men now spent most of their time indoors, lying in their beds for as many as fourteen hours a day trying to keep warm. Still, the expedition seems at no time to have been threatened with destruction.

March brought the caribou back. Roused from their lethargy, the men busied themselves hunting and preparing for the spring travelling. Rae knew from his experience the previous year that ice conditions in Committee Bay would not allow him to skirt the coast by boat. Instead he manufactured two sledges out of material from the boats and purchased dogs from the local natives to pull them.

On April 5, Rae left Fort Hope with four of his men, led by an Inuit guide. "We were accompanied by two sledges, each drawn by four dogs, on which our luggage and provisions were stowed. Our stores consisted of three bags of pemmican, seventy reindeer tongues, one half-hundred weight of flour, some tea, chocolate, and sugar, and a little alcohol and oil for fuel." After crossing the isthmus, they travelled up the west side of Committee Bay. By day they trekked over the frozen surface of the bay, keeping a short distance out from the shore, where ice which had broken against the beach piled up and made the going more difficult. Each evening they made a snowhouse in which to sleep. In order to save precious fuel they slept with kettles of snow beside them under their blankets; during the night it thawed and was ready for drinking in the morning. Cutting overland to Pelly Bay, on April 18 the small party reached their destination—Lord Mayor Bay on the eastern side of Boothia. Here the Rosses had been frozen in for three winters during their dramatic voyage of 1829-33. Because he saw unbroken coastline the entire distance, Rae confirmed that there was no strait separating Boothia from the mainland. Unless the Rosses had missed a passage farther north (which in fact they had, but this would not be learned for several years yet), Boothia was a narrow, unbroken spike of land projecting well to the north of the rest of the coast. Any navigable passage would only be found to the west of it.

Rae did not actually complete the survey of the coast by travelling all the way to the farthest point reached by Dease and Simpson in 1839. However, he proved that the two points were not joined by water, which was the important issue. Retracing his tracks to Fort Hope, where he arrived May 5, he now took up the second objective of his expedition, to reconnoitre the western side of Melville Peninsula all the way to Fury and Hecla Strait. Edward Parry had journeyed to the western end of this frozen strait in 1822, but the farther side of the peninsula was unknown to Europeans, and on May 13 Rae and six companions set out to explore it.

Because the sledges proved hard to manage in the broken ice along the shore, the men carried their supplies on their backs this time. Walking presented its own difficulties, of course. "At one moment we sank nearly waist-deep in snow, at another we were up to our knees in salt water, and then again on a piece of ice so slippery that, with our wet and frozen shoes, it was impossible to keep from falling." Along the way Rae managed to drop a caribou with a bullet through the head. This was a welcome change from pemmican and flour mixed in cold water, and the party paused to feast. Much of the meat was cached for the return trip, but a gourmet soup was made by boiling the contents of the animal's stomach in water, followed by another soup of blood, brains, and meat scraps.

On May 28 Rae decided he hadn't the provisions to continue. He turned back just sixteen kilometres from Fury and Hecla Strait. In two overland voyages remarkable for the distances they covered, on foot, relying on indigenous means of survival, Rae and his men forged the final link in the chain of discoveries which revealed at last the extent and shape of the most northerly coast of the American continent. His task complete, he launched his boats and sailed away from Repulse Bay.

The gradual discovery of the Arctic coastline was accomplished by European manpower for European purposes but in the end it was a triumph for Inuit know-how and indigenous travel skills. It is proper to recognize the bravery of a Franklin, the zeal of a Simpson, the resourcefulness of a Rae; but none of these men would have succeeded in their purpose without the assistance of the Indians who hunted food for them and the Inuit who shared their knowledge. As successive explorers tried their hand at solving the puzzle of the Northwest Passage, they adopted means of travel which relied more and more on native models. John Rae was the end-product of this process. Travelling with only a few companions, unburdened by bulky supplies of food, Rae accomplished his objectives on snowshoe and sled, built shelters out of rock and snow, and survived by eating animals he killed himself and cooked in the age-old manner of arctic inhabitants. He benefitted from Inuit help in the obvious sense that a local man was his guide, but more importantly he relied on Inuit example to develop a new way of travelling for explorers in the North—fast, light, and self-reliant. Later, Rae's techniques would be used by other explorers to complete the discovery of the Canadian North.

For the moment, however, John Rae's expedition to Repulse Bay marks the end of an era in northern exploration. The Northwest Passage was no longer the only magnet attracting Europeans into the Arctic. That venerable secret, still undisclosed, was superseded by another, more pressing mystery. Somewhere in the frozen North, 129 British seamen were lost. They had disappeared in the white vastness without a trace, and for the next dozen years the story of arctic discovery was the story of their fate.

7

Lost and Found:
The Search for Franklin

Following his triumphant return from Canada in 1827, John Franklin discovered that in the peacetime navy heroic service did not necessarily result in steady employment. For almost three years he languished without a command. He married for the second time, his first wife having died while he was absent in the Arctic, and travelled with his bride to several distant countries. Finally, in 1830, he was sent to the Mediterranean to take command of a twenty-six-gun warship. This posting lasted just three and a half years, however, after which he was back in England fretting at the inactivity. Then, in 1836, he was appointed governor to the island colony of Van Diemen's Land, known today as Tasmania. Franklin remained there for seven years until a run-in with another colonial official brought about his recall. As it turned out, he returned to England in 1844 at a very opportune moment. John Barrow, still at the Admiralty after all

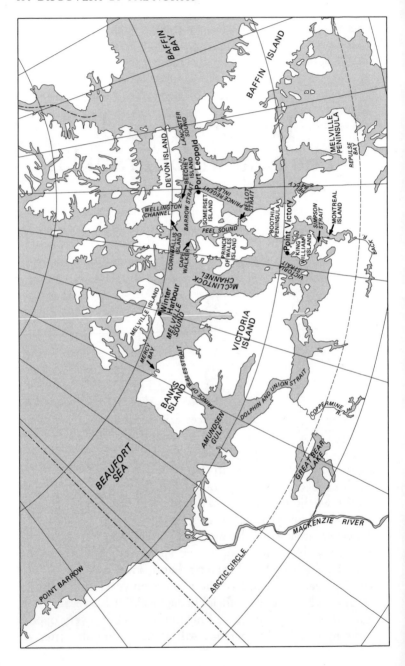

these years, was preparing yet another naval expedition in search of a Northwest Passage. He was determined that this prize should belong to Britain and in his less lucid moments speculated that the trip could be made in just two weeks.

Despite his availability and experience, Franklin was not Barrow's first choice to command the expedition. This honour went to James Fitzjames, a friend of the Barrow family, and then, after it was agreed that he was too young and inexperienced, James Clark Ross was offered the post. But Ross, a natural choice, had promised his wife that he would give up the sea and so command devolved to Franklin. "He's a better man to go than any I know," Edward Parry wrote the Admiralty, "and if you don't let him go the man will die of disappointment."

Franklin was given two vessels, the *Erebus* and the *Terror*, much used to sailing in the ice since they had just returned from a long voyage to Antarctica. As usual, the bow of each vessel was strengthened with timbers to a thickness of over two metres, then sheathed in iron plate. While they were bark-rigged with three masts and would rely on the wind whenever possible, the ships were fitted with small, twenty-horsepower auxiliary steam engines and screw propellers to carry them forward when the breeze failed. Enough provisions were hoisted on board to last for three years, by which time all hands fully expected to be through to the Pacific and probably home again.

It was on a buoyant wave of optimism that the Franklin expedition departed England in June 1845. The one discordant voice belonged to Richard King, second in command to George Back on his descent of the Back River the previous decade. Ever since, King had made himself unpopular by championing further land expeditions and criticizing the naval approach. According to King, never known for his polite language, Barrow had sent Franklin to the Arctic to "form the nucleus of an iceberg" and should have supported the *Erebus* and *Terror* with an overland party from the south. Unhappily, King was all too correct in his prediction, but so disliked that the Admiralty was blind to whatever merit his own proposal might have had.

Franklin's official orders directed him to enter Lancaster Sound, cruise through its western extension, Barrow Strait, then veer generally southwest across a part of the arctic archipelago that was still a complete blank on the map. He was expected to make his way around any land he found there, but if the region proved impossible to navigate he was instructed to turn northward up Wellington Channel in an attempt to reach the open polar sea. In other words, Franklin was asked to close the gap between Lancaster Sound and his own coastal discoveries made two decades before.

Franklin's ships crossed Baffin Bay without any difficulty. Late in July they were encountered by a pair of British whaling vessels and reported everything well. Then they sailed into Lancaster Sound, and were never seen by Europeans again.

Since no one survived Franklin's last expedition, nor did any written account, there is no way of knowing the exact details of the voyage. However, enough information was gathered by searchers after the fact to reconstruct the bare outline of events. The *Erebus* and the *Terror* apparently encountered heavy ice in Barrow Strait blocking their way westward that summer. Turning north as his instructions indicated, Franklin sailed up Wellington Channel for about 240 km before circling across the top of Cornwallis Island and returning to Barrow Strait. Seeking a safe winter harbour, he put in at Beechey Island, a prominent islet with steep shores standing out from the southwest corner of Devon Island. During the winter, three crewmen died of natural causes and were buried on the gravel beach.

The next summer, 1846, Franklin once again attempted to sail to the west but, frustrated by ice, he made his way instead down Peel Sound to the south. Ordinarily this narrow passage is choked with ice but Franklin found it open and navigable. Perhaps he congratulated himself as he looked ahead to a rapid conclusion of his voyage. If so, it was a cruel joke. Peel Sound was a seductive trap from which there was no escape. Carrying the ships southward, it led them across the broad mouth of

McClintock Channel, down which the grinding flow of the polar ice pack follows its unrelenting course. Once the *Erebus* and *Terror* were mired in the ice off King William Island, their fate was sealed. Subsequent explorers following in Franklin's track would know to keep to the eastern side of the island and follow the relatively ice-free interior passages next to the continental shore. But Franklin could not know this, and so he paid the price of the pioneer.

Imprisoned in the ice of Victoria Strait, several kilometres offshore from King William Island, the sailors settled in for their second winter in the Arctic. The region in which they found themselves was not productive of much game and they were cut off from the shore by hummocky ice anyway, so the crews had to rely for food on the provisions they had brought with them. The following May, 1847, Lieutenant Graham Gore commanded a sled journey to King William Island. Proceeding to the south coast of the island, he probably reached Simpson Strait, already known to explorers, thereby closing the final gap in the Northwest Passage.

In June Franklin died of unspecified causes and command of the expedition fell to F. R. M. Crozier. "The spring of 1847 found them within 90 miles of the known sea off the coast of America," wrote the man who eventually discovered their fate, "and to men who had already in two seasons sailed over 500 miles of previously unexplored waters, how confident must they then have felt that that forthcoming navigable season of 1847 would see their ships pass over so short an intervening space!"

But it was not to be. During the summer the ships could not make any headway against the ice which held them, and the crews were forced to endure yet another frozen winter. By this time scurvy was epidemic as foodstocks dwindled. Escape was impossible during the dark winter, but when spring arrived Crozier decided to make a desperate bid for safety. Already two dozen members of the expedition were dead; it would be suicide to remain much longer at the ships.

On April 22, 1848, after nineteen months in the ice, the 109 survivors abandoned the *Erebus* and the *Terror*. Towing boats mounted on sledges, they trekked across the frozen strait to King William Island, then turned south across the island toward the continent. They were making for the mouth of the Back River, perhaps to meet the rescuers they hoped were coming for them, perhaps in search of caribou to hunt. They never made it. Weakened by scurvy, inexperienced at overland travel, ill-equipped to face the rigours of the journey and overburdened with heavy loads from the ships, the sailors one by one lay down in the snow and died. Some sat propped against a rock; others took to their tents and never got up again; others simply collapsed as they walked along. Even in their distress sailors at first paused to bury their shipmates, but eventually there was no strength left and the white arctic beach was strewn with corpses. A party of the strongest managed to cross Simpson Strait and camp for the last time in a small bay on the continental shore, now called Starvation Cove. And this is where the Franklin expedition ended, as a long silence closed over them.

Concern over the safety of Franklin and his men developed slowly in England. Arctic expeditions were commonly away for at least one year, often two, and there was the example of John Ross, who had emerged from the North after an unprecedented four winters in the ice. Ironically, it was Ross himself who first raised the alarm about Franklin. The irascible old explorer had objected to the expedition from the start, arguing his favourite theory that arctic ships should be lightweight and of shallow draft for better manoeuvring between the ice pack and the shore, not large, heavy vessels like the *Erebus* and the *Terror*. But he assured Franklin before he departed that "I shall volunteer to look for you, if you are not heard of in February, 1847." A man of his word, Ross, now approaching seventy years of age, delayed his retirement from the navy to keep himself available for duty and, when his worst fears were realized, he applied to the Admiralty early in 1847 for a ship to go in search of Franklin. Admiralty officials, however, did not share Ross's anxiety. They dismissed his offer, suggesting that the old commander was simply looking for an excuse to get back in the limelight.

In the open season of 1847 Franklin was dead, but most of his men were still alive. If a ship had been sent it might possibly have located the *Erebus* and the *Terror* before they were abandoned the following spring. Such a rescue was at least possible, if extremely improbable. Certainly the decision not to send a ship ended all hope for the lost men. By the time the first ships would sail in search of them they would all be dead.

Speculation about the whereabouts of Franklin centred on two questions: firstly, what route did he follow; and secondly, if he was in trouble, where would he attempt to make his escape. The search, when it did get under way, was vastly complicated by differences of opinion on both matters. Franklin's instructions directed him south and west of Lancaster Sound. Did he follow these instructions or did he follow the alternative they contained, north up Wellington Channel? Perhaps he had succeeded in crossing the archipelago and now was caught somewhere near its western edge, in which case rescue via Bering Strait seemed the sensible plan. If the *Erebus* and the *Terror* were wrecked, would Franklin lead his men back toward Lancaster Sound where the whaling fleet cruised each summer, as John Ross had done? Or would he make for the mainland and one of the rivers leading to the south?

Another irony of the Franklin episode was the fact that at the very beginning someone accurately answered all these questions. Richard King believed that the expedition was inextricably mired in the ice somewhere to the west of Boothia where rescue ships would have little chance of reaching them. He proposed that vessels be sent up Lancaster Sound to put out food caches along the shore, while an overland expedition, naturally led by himself, should be dispatched down the Back River into the archipelago to locate Franklin and lead him to safety. If King's proposal had been acted upon no lives would have been saved; it was even then too late for that. However, he might have learned the sad fate of the expedition several years earlier and thus prevented the suffering and expense of the many rescue attempts which followed. Unhappily, King was not popular with the naval establishment. His arctic experience amounted to just one land expedition, which had not accomplished very much. It was all too easy to dismiss him, as the Admiralty did, as an irritating amateur who had made the Back River his hobby horse and was trying to ride it to public prominence. "A person who omits no opportunity of directing public attention upon himself," sniffed Edward Parry. Anyway, King had had the tactlessness to predict openly that Franklin would come to grief, and the Admiralty hated him for being able to say he told them so. There would be no descent of the Back River.

The expeditions which the Admiralty did send out in 1848 were planned to satisfy several different theories about Franklin's whereabouts. James Clark Ross was coaxed back into uniform to take two ships up Lancaster Sound beyond Boothia. John Richardson and John Rae were hurried off to America to travel down the Mackenzie toward the Victoria Island area, while another ship sailed for the Pacific and Bering Strait to watch the western exit for any sign of the missing expedition. The variety of these expeditions emphasizes the monumental difficulty of the task facing the Admiralty. Franklin had disappeared into a white vastness, only part of which was even on the map. Given weather and ice conditions, a systematic search of the area by ship was impossible, or at least would take years, and time was not a luxury the Admiralty had much of. It seems amusing today to read about searchers launching small balloons with time fuses to drop messages, or trapping foxes and releasing them wearing metal collars with messages attached. Someone even suggested sending gangs of convicted criminals to carry out the search on foot. Such desperate ideas were a response to the huge space and the limited means of covering it.

The first rescue expeditions obtained negligible results. After being delayed in the ice of Baffin Bay so long he could accomplish almost nothing the first season, James Ross wintered at Port Leopold near the top of Prince Regent Inlet. While ships were useful for surveying the shoreline for cairns or wreckage, open season was limited, and it was therefore by spring sledging that most of the search would be conducted in the years ahead. In the spring of 1849, Ross dispatched two sledge parties across Somerset Island to Peel Sound, a narrow channel which the seamen had not known existed. As he followed it southward, Ross of course did not know that he was following the route actually taken by Franklin three years earlier. It is yet another irony that the first rescue expedition to come searching should have stumbled so unwittingly on the correct trail, and a tragedy that Ross turned back without realizing this. Ross's bad luck continued that summer. His ships could not get away from Port Leopold until late in August, and then they were trapped in the ice in Lancaster Sound and carried helplessly away from the search area out into Baffin Bay.

James Ross's arrival back in England with so little to report aroused deep disappointment and anxiety for the safety of Franklin and his men. The British public, and the Admiralty itself, was learning just how formidable the Canadian Arctic was, that it could defeat so easily the leading naval explorer of the day. Obviously, rescue missions on a grander scale were required. The season of 1850, therefore, saw a total of six expeditions consisting of a dozen ships and about 450 men launched into the North. One of these vessels would return in a few short months; another would not return at all. None would locate the missing seamen.

The expeditions of 1850 followed the pattern set two years earlier. The two vessels James Ross had commanded, the *Enterprise* and the *Investigator*, were sent to Bering Strait under Captain Richard Collinson. The rest concentrated their search in Lancaster Sound, hoping to discover some clue as to the direction Franklin had taken. At last, late in August, the first clue was found. As the ship *Assistance* sailed close by Beechey Island, a lookout spied a cairn standing out atop the high shoreline. Captain Erasmus Ommaney landed and discovered traces of an expedition which must have been Franklin's since, other than Edward Parry, no one else had managed to penetrate so far up the strait. Later that season several of the rescue vessels congregated at Beechey, where further searches turned up evidence that the island had been used as a winter harbour. Discarded meat tins, pieces of rope and cloth, sledge tracks, the ruins of buildings, graves of the three crewmen who died—all proved conclusively that Franklin had passed the winter of 1845–46 at Beechey. But where did he go from there? "There was a sickening anxiety of the heart as one involuntarily clutched at every relic they of Franklin's squadron had left behind," wrote Sherard Osborn, captain of one of the ships, "in the vain hope that some clue as to the route they had taken hence might be found." But no clue was found and the rescue vessels went into winter harbour themselves without any idea where to take up the search the next year.

As a result, twenty-one sledges were sent out in every conceivable direction in the spring of 1851. One party, led by Lieutenant Francis Leopold McClintock, travelled west to Melville Island, the first Europeans to reach Winter Harbour since Parry's visit in 1819–20. Another party crossed Barrow Strait to Cape Walker at the northeast corner of Prince of Wales Island. When Franklin left England, Cape Walker was the last known landmark filled in on the map in this direction; beyond it he would plunge into the unknown regions of the central archipelago. It was assumed that he would have left a message in a cairn there, if he had got so far. But the searchers found nothing, either at the cape or along the coast of Prince of Wales Island. They returned to their ships convinced that no ships could have successfully penetrated the thick ice they had seen; Franklin must have gone in another direction.

This unfortunate conclusion was reinforced by another group of sleds, which travelled north up Wellington Channel. Here, on the coast of Cornwallis Island, two pieces of wood were found which seemed to indicate the *Erebus* and the *Terror* had been in this direction, which of course they had. What the searchers could not know was that Franklin had explored Wellington Channel before he wintered at Beechey Island, not after. In sum, the overwhelming opinion formed from these expeditions, which returned to England in the fall of 1851, was that further searches must focus on the region north of Lancaster Sound, where Franklin was not, instead of to the south, where he was.

While Admiralty sledges were busy combing the shores of

Lancaster Sound, and jumping to erroneous conclusions, the man who might have turned the entire search in the right direction was carrying out his own reconnaissance far to the south. John Rae had been sent to the Mackenzie River with John Richardson early in 1848 on one of the earliest search expeditions. Initially the two explorers accomplished very little. Richardson returned to England, and Rae took up his duties as a trader with the Hudson's Bay Company. However, in 1850 Rae was sent back to the Arctic to resume the search. Departing his winter base at Great Bear Lake early the following spring, Rae hiked to the northern coast, crossed the frozen sheet of Dolphin and Union Strait and inspected over a thousand kilometres of the southern coastline of Victoria Island. Once spring had passed and the ice had thawed, Rae switched to boat travel and continued his survey to the east, eventually arriving at the southeast corner of the island, where the heavy ice of Victoria Strait blocked his progress, the same heavy ice which had trapped the *Erebus* and the *Terror* five years earlier not seventy kilometres away. Rae stood on the high shore of Victoria Island, gazing across the strait, and waited for conditions to improve so that he might cross to King William Island. But time ran out and he was forced to turn back.

At Parker Bay on the south shore of Victoria Island, his party found two pieces of wood which came unmistakably from a British vessel, probably Franklin's. One piece resembled the end of a small flagstaff; the other was part of an oak stanchion. These pieces of debris might have suggested that Franklin had sailed south of Lancaster Sound after all, but only if they could be positively identified as belonging to the *Erebus* or *Terror* and this was never done, despite the fact that the Admiralty canvassed the opinions of all its arctic veterans. Many British ships had visited the Arctic since 1818; theoretically, any of them might have lost the pieces. Rae himself did not conclude anything from his discovery. Given the developing consensus of opinion in Britain in favour of extending the search northward, the implications of the find were ignored.

In England the search for Franklin and his men fired the

public imagination. Newspapers and magazines overflowed with rumours and advice, all expressed in the most heroic language. The search was "full of wild grandeur and a profound pathos," one typical quarterly told its readers; "fancy these men in their adamantine prison, wherever it may be, chained up by the Polar Spirit." Encouraging this grandiloquent view was the figure of Lady Jane Franklin, the missing hero's wife. They had married in 1828, shortly after Franklin returned from his second expedition to the Canadian Arctic, and they had been together through the restless years of under-employment and the tour of duty in Tasmania. Resourceful, outspoken, and totally devoted, Lady Jane became the focus of public sympathy not just for her apparent bereavement but even more for the way she refused to accept it. Even when all hope of rescue was gone she persisted in the search long after others had given up, wanting definite proof of exactly what happened to her husband and the men who perished with him. With no store of family wealth to draw on, Lady Franklin had to appeal to the Admiralty and the public at large to carry out her plans. In this she was not shy and managed to raise enough money through public subscription to dispatch several ships on what she called "our sacred cause."

Along with the celebrity, Lady Franklin attracted a good number of clairvoyants and mediums who claimed to have information about her husband's whereabouts. Among them was an old sea-captain named William Coppin, whose recently deceased young daughter apparently appeared before the amazed eyes of his other children to announce that Franklin was still alive and marooned in Prince Regent Inlet. Unwilling to neglect any clue, Lady Franklin relayed this news to the captain of one of her vessels just as he set off for the Arctic, but he found the story "more surprising than sensible."

Despite Captain Coppin's daughter, Lady Jane by the end of 1851 shared the growing consensus that the *Erebus* and the *Terror* should be sought north of Lancaster Sound. "I am persuaded now that it is pretty well proved that my husband could not have penetrated south west," she wrote, "but that he has taken the only alternative their instructions presented him by going up the Wellington Channel." In accordance with this opinion, in 1852 the Admiralty organized another large relief expedition consisting of four ships, two of them steam-powered, supported by a supply vessel. Initially the entire squadron was ordered up Wellington Channel, but on second thought it seemed wiser to divert two of the ships directly west toward Melville Island. It had been two years since anything had been heard of the *Investigator* and the *Enterprise*, the two vessels which had sailed early in 1850 to prowl the western Arctic via Bering Strait. Melville Island seemed a sensible place to go looking for them. The search for Franklin had become the search for his rescuers as well.

By the time anyone came looking for them, the *Investigator* and the *Enterprise* were lodged in ice prisons almost three hundred kilometres apart with as little idea of where the other was as any of their would-be rescuers. Captain Richard Collinson in the *Enterprise* commanded the expedition. But as the ships sped toward their appointed rendezvous in Alaska, Robert McClure, captain of the *Investigator*, had slipped his leash, arrived at Bering Strait well in advance of his consort, and plunged into the Arctic on his own. Afterwards there was much debate whether McClure was motivated by unscrupulous ambition, negligence, or honourable zeal. It was highly irregular of him to risk permanent separation from his sister ship and highly ingenuous to claim that he believed Collinson was probably in front of him and he simply was trying to catch up. But the Arctic had shown that hesitation and delay brought few rewards; there were naval men missing in the ice, perhaps in peril of their lives, and he could not relieve them hanging about waiting for a tardy commander. On August 7, 1850, McClure and the sixty-five men of the *Investigator* sailed around Point Barrow, the top of Alaska, and headed eastward along the coast into the Beaufort Sea. It was not a happy ship—the captain quarrelled with his officers constantly and flogged his men mercilessly—but it was destined to make a great discovery.

The Beaufort Sea was at this time completely unknown to European seamen. Franklin and Thomas Simpson had cruised in boats along its shore, but no ship had ventured into it. It was covered for most of the year by the polar ice pack, which retreated briefly each summer from the coast of the continent, opening a corridor of water full of gravel shoals and stray pieces of ice. It was down this treacherous channel that McClure navigated the *Investigator.* He described the scene: "On the one hand, lay a low and dangerous coast, devoid of any shelter or haven, on the other a barrier of packed ice formed of great floe pieces and hummocks; the intervening space also being much covered with stray masses, so dense and heavy in their nature as to cause the vessel to tremble in every timber whenever she unavoidably struck any of them." His position was made even more perilous by the shifting wind, which at any time might drive the pack down against the coast breaking the ship to splinters on the rocks.

After an anxious run down the coast, McClure arrived at reasonably open water off the mouth of the Mackenzie River. Continuing eastward, he passed into what is now called Amundsen Gulf, all the time seeking a safe place to shelter his vessel for the coming winter. But ice began to force him away from the shore and he veered northward, picking his way through the broken pack and straying into what appeared to be a narrow inlet. As he proceeded up the inlet McClure realized that it actually was a strait leading away to the northeast. "Can it be possible that this water communicates with Barrow's Strait, and shall prove to be the long-sought North-west Passage?" he asked his journal. The *Investigator* was cruising up Prince of Wales Strait between the high shores of Banks and Victoria islands. This strait does indeed connect with Barrow Strait, but the thick ice of Melville Sound intervenes to make it virtually impossible for a ship, especially one powered by sail, to pass through.

Toward the end of September the *Investigator* reached the top of Prince of Wales Strait; McClure gazed upon the vast fields of ice ahead and knew he could not go on, at least that season. Unwilling to give up any of the ground he had gained so laboriously, the captain did not retreat in search of a harbour but instead decided to prepare the ship to spend the winter adrift in the ice. This decision exposed the *Investigator* to even greater risks than a usual winter spent in the Arctic. Out in the open pack without shelter from the wind and the moving ice, a ship was completely helpless. The thick pack held it like a vice, tightening in wind and storm until the hull cracked and the decks buckled, then easing with the return of calmer weather. As the ice drifted aimlessly back and forth, it carried the vessel along and at any time could throw it onto an island or smash it against a bold cliff face. And then there were the bergs, gigantic mountains of ice which came sliding through the pack like a hot knife through butter, threatening to overwhelm any ship lying paralyzed in their path.

October was the worst month. The deep freeze had not yet set in and the ice heaved and cracked in response to wind and current. During this month in 1850 the *Investigator* was carried back down Prince of Wales Strait, miraculously surviving a series of storms and crushes. Johann Miertsching, a Moravian missionary who had been brought along as an Inuit interpreter, described one close call.

> The past night was the most horrible that we have yet experienced....For seventeen hours we stood ready on the deck where each moment appeared to be our last; great massive pieces of ice three and four times the size of the ship were pushed one on top of another and under continuing pressure forced into a towering heap which could then come tumbling down with a thunderous roar. In the thick of this ice-revolution lay the ship, thrown now on one broadside, now on the other, then again heaved up out of the water, and, when the towering ice collapsed, the ship came crashing down into the sea. The ship's beams were so sprung apart that the tarred oakum was falling out of the seams; even the casks in the hold began to crack....Had we seen a chance of reaching land across this surging ice-field, not a man would have remained on the ship.

Since they could not escape the men did the next best thing: they raided the stores and got falling-down drunk.

The storm ended with an eerie abruptness. "On board

amongst the crew there is a hush," wrote Miertsching, "the men behave as if frightened and few words are exchanged; they all seem to have suffered a shock and to have no spirit left." Late in October the ice settled down, and it was safe to leave the ship. McClure took six men with a sledge on a hike to the top of the strait. At the northeast corner of Banks Island, the party climbed a high hill from where the sailors could look across Melville Sound to the low, shadowy bulk of Melville Island about one hundred kilometres away. Across this same ice-filled channel Edward Parry had looked thirty years before from the opposite direction; it was the final gap in another Northwest Passage, the second to be discovered by European seamen, and McClure was determined to cross it in his ship the next season.

Back at the *Investigator* life slipped into a winter routine unbroken by incident or accident. Decks were roofed over with canvas and the walls were packed with snow to a thickness of 2.5 m. "Life on board ship is, so to speak, a sort of machine," lamented the bored Miertsching, "one day is like another; every task is done every day at the same time in the same way." Meals assumed the same monotony. Breakfast consisted of a cup of cocoa and a piece of salt pork; at mid-day the men were treated to vegetables with another piece of salt meat; supper was a cup of black tea and more meat, followed by a ration of grog. The sun disappeared November 11, not to reappear until the following February, and during the dark season this diet was not supplemented by fresh food. Once the sun returned, however, the men were out hunting on the nearby islands almost every day. In mid-April, 1851, the search for Franklin was taken up by three sledge parties, which examined the shores of Banks and Victoria islands in all directions. By early June they were back at the ship with nothing to report.

McClure still hoped to penetrate Melville Sound and, when at last the long winter ended and the *Investigator* again sailed free before the wind, he steered for the north end of Prince of Wales Strait. However, once again he was frustrated by the heavy ice stream. A less persistent commander might have gone home, but McClure had other plans. Running back down the strait, he sailed underneath Banks Island and north again up its western side, thinking to approach Melville Sound from another angle. McClure's audacity was breathtaking, if his judgement a little rash. At first, conditions favoured the project, but as the *Investigator* approached the northwest corner of Banks Island the shore steepened into precipitous cliffs and the ice pressed in close, leaving only a narrow lane of water for the ship to follow. A wall of ice more than three metres·high loomed above the decks; at times the outrigging scraped the cold barrier on one side and the cliff face on the other. The position of the ship was extremely vulnerable, since at any time the ice might crush it, but there was no room to turn around and so they went on, boats towing the vessel along the island's north shore.

In early September the *Investigator* was actually squeezed out of the water onto a floe, where it lay on its side like a beached whale. After several days in this position, a breeze from the south began to drive the ice away from the coast, carrying the ship with it. McClure managed to free the vessel by blowing up its bed of ice, and the *Investigator* resumed its slow crawl along the coast. Huge pieces of the pack heaved and groaned as they piled up on the beach or smashed together in thunderous collisions. The state of mind of the men, who every moment expected the ship to be wrecked and themselves cast up on the barren shore, can only be imagined.

This incredible voyage reached its climax one day in the third week of September. A dense fog obscured visibility almost totally; snow was falling thickly. The *Investigator* was under sail following a thread-like channel of water which seemed to open miraculously, then close behind the ship. "All was ice ahead and not a spoonful of water to be seen," recalled Miertsching, "and yet the ship was speeding on without hindrance..." Suddenly a tall floe appeared out of the fog directly ahead. Rushing to avert a collision, all hands were amazed to see the ice open like a curtain to allow them through. So nerve-wracking and inexplicable was the experience that a shaken lookout climbed down from the crow's nest and refused to go aloft again. It was as if the sailors were riding a ghost ship.

On September 24, the remarkable voyage came to an end. The ship was forced into a deep bay on the north coast of Banks Island, and McClure decided that he would not try to get back into the ice stream. For once he seems to have put the safety of his men ahead of his own ambition to cross the Northwest Passage. The bay, called Mercy by the grateful captain, would be home to the expedition for the next year and a half, and proved to be the final resting place of the *Investigator*.

At first Mercy Bay seemed a fortunate winter harbour. Caribou were plentiful in the broad valleys along the shoreline and, along with small birds and hare, provided the fresh meat which probably saved the lives of the stranded sailors. There was the usual grumbling and sickness, but on the whole the crew came through the winter of 1851–52 in good spirits, probably because they looked forward to getting out of the ice the next season. In April 1852 McClure, along with a sledge party of six men, crossed Melville Sound on foot to visit Winter Harbour. He expected to find a cache of provisions there; he hoped to find a ship; what he did find was a simple message informing him that Lieutenant McClintock had been there the previous year and that the nearest vessel was probably five hundred kilometres away. When McClure learned that the rescuers he was counting on had come and gone, he broke down and wept.

Back at the *Investigator* the expedition waited impatiently for ice in the bay to break up, but it never did. Days passed slowly with nothing to do but watch anxiously for some movement in the pack. "No immediate work can be found for these men," wrote the missionary Miertsching, "who creep around with drooping heads and empty stomachs." Wild sorrel was gathered from the shore and fed to the men; nevertheless, they were beginning to sicken with scurvy. By September it was clear there would be no escape. Rations had already been reduced to conserve supplies; they could not be cut back any further. As it was, the men were slowly starving to death.

Constantly hungry, they dug in the garbage heap on shore for scraps of food or ate raw the few animals they killed instead of returning them to the ship to be shared. A deep depression stole over the crew as winter progressed, combining with famine to leave the men feeble and dispirited. "Instead of the once cheery and active sailors," Miertsching observed, "now one only sees creeping about the shrunken forms of men who have no desire but to sleep." At the end of February one-third of the crew were in hospital. The minds of two sailors snapped under the strain, and during the long nights the others lay in their beds listening to the unearthly moans and howls of their unfortunate companions.

Captain McClure was faced with a difficult decision. Obviously his entire crew could not spend yet another winter in the Arctic; if the *Investigator* did not get free in the summer of 1853 they would all perish. However, he could not desert the vessel in the spring in order to lead the men on a trek overland to safety in case the ice did break up and the ship was able to complete the voyage. McClure decided on a compromise. He told the men that a skeleton crew of the healthiest among them would remain at the ship to sail it home if conditions permitted. The rest would be sent away with sledges in two parties, one eastward toward Lancaster Sound and one southward across Banks Island toward the mainland and the Mackenzie River. It was a desperate gamble, the men being much reduced by disease and hunger, but the only apparent alternative was to face certain starvation together.

The date set for the departure of the sleds was April 15. On April 5, the first member of the crew died. The next day McClure was walking on the ice near the ship with one of his officers, discussing how to prepare a grave in frozen ground, when an unidentified figure was seen approaching from the head of the bay. "From his pace and gestures we both naturally supposed at first that he was some one of our party pursued by a bear, but as we approached him doubts arose as to who it could be," McClure recalled in his journal.

When within about two hundred yards of us, this strange figure threw up his arms, and made gesticulations resembling those used by Esquimaux, besides shouting, at the top of his voice, words which, from the wind and intense excitement of the moment, sounded like a wild screech; and this brought us both fairly to a stand-still. The stranger came quietly on, and we saw that his face was black as ebony, and really at the moment we might be pardoned for wondering whether he was a denizen of this or the other world...: as it was, we gallantly stood our ground, and, had the skies fallen upon us, we could hardly have been more astonished than when the dark-faced stranger called out,—"I'm Lieutenant Pim, late of the *Herald*, and now in the *Resolute*. Captain Kellett is in her at Dealey Island!"

At this dramatic statement, that the stranger standing before them was actually a brother officer in the Royal Navy, that an Admiralty vessel was waiting at Melville Island, the wretched crew of the *Investigator* was transformed. "The news flew with lightning rapidity," McClure continued; "the ship was all in commotion; the sick, forgetful of their maladies, leapt from their hammocks; the artificers dropped their tools, and the lower deck was cleared of men; for they all rushed for the hatchway to be assured that a stranger was actually amongst them...."

The rescue vessel that relieved McClure was part of the squadron sent to search for John Franklin in 1852. The *Resolute*, along with its steam tender, *Intrepid*, managed to reach Melville Island via Barrow Strait that summer, though instead of wintering at Winter Harbour they put in at Dealey Island about sixty-five kilometres back down the coast. In October sledge parties were dispatched to put down supply depots for the major search, which would begin the following spring. It was one of these parties which discovered the message left by McClure when he had crossed to Winter Harbour earlier in the year. It was too late to attempt to reach the *Investigator* that fall, but early in March 1853 Lieutenant Bedford Pim made the journey, luckily arriving just nine days before so many of the men of the *Investigator* were scheduled to leave on their own desperate journeys.

McClure was at first reluctant to abandon his ship now that help had come. Perhaps he still harboured the hope that he would sail through the Northwest Passage; perhaps he was taking into account the severity with which the Admiralty viewed a captain who returned without his vessel. Whatever his motives, McClure wanted an explicit order from a senior officer to quit Mercy Bay. Once Captain Kellett at Dealey Island saw the state of the *Investigator* men, the order was quickly given. Two more had died in recent days and a doctor could not find even ten men strong enough to sail the ship. At last the *Investigator* was abandoned by the last of its crew on June 3.

Miertsching described the arrival of the survivors at Dealey Island after their march across Melville Sound. "Two sick men were lashed on to each of the four sledges; others, utterly without strength, were supported by comrades who still preserved a little vigour; others again held on to and leaned on the sledges, and these were drawn by men so unsteady on their feet that every five minutes they would fall and be unable to rise without the help of their comrades...." The least fit were helped to continue their journey by sledge to the rendezvous at Beechey Island where they hitched a ride on a supply ship, arriving back in England in October 1853. After three hundred years of trying, the first Europeans had finally traversed the Northwest Passage.

McClure and the others who had stayed behind at Dealey Island were not yet out of harm's way. Passengers now aboard the *Resolute* and the *Intrepid*, they were trapped along with the rest when these ships failed to get out of Lancaster Sound that season. Incredibly, the men of the *Investigator* were forced to spend yet another winter, their fourth, in the Arctic. Next spring a message arrived from the other two vessels which had sailed with Captain Kellett's. The entire squadron was under the command of Edward Belcher, an unsavoury person known for brutality to his men and spitefulness toward his fellow officers. Having spent two winters himself trapped in Wellington Channel, Belcher was determined not to have to pass a third. At first his orders were equivocal; Kellett was to meet him that summer with all his men at Beechey Island. Did Belcher mean that the ships should be abandoned, Kellett inquired, not believing that such a drastic measure could possibly be contemplated. But Belcher shot back an order that left no question; the ships were to be deserted and all hands must make their way to the rendezvous by sled. The commander also gave up his two vessels, and the entire complement of men was carried home by a trio of supply vessels. Belcher faced a court martial for his conduct but was acquitted.

There was an ignominious footnote to this episode. Captain Kellett's ship, the *Resolute*, was not crushed in the ice after all; instead it drifted slowly out of Lancaster Sound and down into Davis Strait, where it was rescued a year later by an American whaler, who towed it home to New England. The United States Congress bought the salvaged derelict for forty thousand dollars, refitted it, and magnanimously returned it to Great Britain as a gift. Years later when the *Resolute* was broken up, some of the timbers were made into an oak table which was presented by the British government to the American president. For some time the table gathered dust in a storeroom, but during the term of John F. Kennedy it was rescued and put on display in the White House.

During the search for Franklin the Arctic often resembled one of those long, comic hallways lined with doors through which people appear and disappear as they attempt to find one another, always narrowly failing to make contact. No voyage conformed to this image more precisely than that of the *Enterprise*, sister ship of the unlucky *Investigator*. The *Enterprise* arrived in the western Arctic in the summer of 1850 too late to follow the intrepid McClure into the Beaufort Sea. Captain Richard Collinson retired to Hong Kong for the winter but returned the next year and successfully negotiated the perilous run down the coast of Alaska and the Yukon into Amundsen Gulf. Like McClure, Collinson located and entered Prince of Wales Strait, just ten days after his colleague had sailed out of the strait on his way around Banks Island. Unaware that he was travelling in the wake of the *Investigator*, Collinson took the *Enterprise* north up the strait until he too was halted by the impenetrable ice barrier in Melville Sound. Returning south, he unknowingly began to follow McClure on a circuit of Banks Island but once again had to fall back in the face of extremely heavy ice.

Collinson wintered his ship on the west coast of Victoria Island, from where he made the customary spring sledge journeys in search of traces of Franklin. Then he sailed through Dolphin and Union Strait along the south shore of Victoria Island, the first ship to penetrate so deeply into these coastal waters. Now he was following a shoreline traced by John Rae just a year earlier. The *Enterprise* stopped for the winter of 1852–53 at Cambridge Bay. It was now getting very close to the spot where the answer to the Franklin puzzle lay. But in the spring of 1853 Collinson decided to investigate the west side of Victoria Strait, not knowing that Rae had already done so. Had he used the sledging season to explore the opposite side of the strait he probably would have found the remains of the missing expedition. As it was, he found nothing but a cairn built by Rae. A disappointed Collinson sailed out of the archipelago that summer and returned to England. While he was on his way home, word of Franklin's fate finally reached the outside world.

After his expedition to Victoria Island in 1851, John Rae had given up the Franklin search. His forte was overland and coastal travel, and he seems to have believed that the missing ships would be found deeper in the archipelago, if they were found at all. However, Rae did not give up arctic exploration entirely. Franklin aside, there were still unknown areas of the North to investigate. For instance, the west coast of Boothia had not been fully surveyed and there was yet the question of King William's Land—was it an island or was it attached to Boothia? To settle these matters Rae embarked on his fourth excursion into the Arctic. It is the final irony of the Franklin episode that the fate of the expedition was discovered first by a man who was not even looking for it.

Rae arrived at his familiar wintering spot at Repulse Bay in

Hudson Bay in the fall of 1853. The following March, he set off with four companions hauling sledges across Melville Peninsula, overland to Boothia Peninsula, and then up the western coast. Just short of Bellot Strait the party was delayed by poor weather and had to turn back before completing its objective. Rae succeeded in proving once and for all that Boothia and King William Island were not joined, but when he returned to England that fall he had much more exciting news than that.

During his journey he met several Inuit around Pelly Bay who told him stories they had heard from other native people about a large number of *kabloonas*, white men, having been seen far to the west several years before. Piecing the different information together, Rae came up with a coherent, if imprecise, account. According to the Inuit, one spring four years previous (they were wrong about this; it was actually six years) a group of families hunting seal in the strait off the south shore of King William Island saw a group of about forty Europeans dragging a boat and sledges across the ice. Communicating by sign language, the strangers told the Inuit their ships were wrecked and they were heading for the mainland, where they hoped to find caribou to kill. They looked very weak and hungry and, after purchasing a seal from the Inuit, moved on. Later that spring, the natives told Rae, about thirty-five corpses and some graves were found in the vicinity of Starvation Cove on the mainland side of the strait. "From the mutilated state of many of the bodies," Rae reported, "and the contents of the kettles, it is evident that our wretched Countrymen had been driven to the last dread alternative, as a means of sustaining life."

This suggestion of cannibalism raised a storm of controversy in England when Rae's account became public. Surely British sailors were incapable of such a barbaric act. Rae was rebuked for making accusations based on the evidence of "uncivilized" native people who had not even visited the scene themselves. Charles Dickens, at the height of his popular success, suggested in print that the Inuit had probably murdered the seamen, and there were many who agreed with him. Rae was also criticized for not immediately travelling to the site of the tragedy and making certain of the details himself. Instead, the gossips had it, he hurried off home to claim the reward and the celebrity.

These charges were in the end discounted by the Admiralty, which accepted the substance of his account and awarded Rae and his men ten thousand pounds for discovering the fate of the Franklin expedition. The navy was pleased to be able to write a finish to the protracted search. It had already preoccupied an inordinate number of ships and men; now that the Crimean War had broken out, the Admiralty had other uses for its personnel. When Lady Franklin requested that another expedition be sent to collect whatever records and remains of her husband's ill-fated voyage might still exist, she was courteously turned down. Quite naturally the Admiralty saw no point in risking the loss of more lives when none could possibly be saved. Lady Franklin, however, persisted. Raising money by public subscription, she purchased a 160-tonne steam yacht built by a British nobleman for luxury cruising and engaged Captain Francis Leopold McClintock to command the expedition. The *Fox*, with a crew of twenty-five and provisions to last twenty-eight months, sailed from England on July 1, 1857.

For an expedition which would accomplish so much, it began by accomplishing very little. Following the traditional route up the coast of Greenland and across the top of Baffin Bay, the *Fox* became trapped in the ice as it tried to work its way westward. Summer faded into autumn and there was no release. The little yacht would have to spend the winter out in the pack, at least 150 km from land, where contending floes crash together and gales sweep unimpeded down from the Pole. During the winter the ice in Baffin Bay drifts southward into Davis Strait, and it carried the *Fox* with it. Miraculously preserved from destruction, McClintock and his men were not released by the pack until late in April 1858, after a drift of 2000 km lasting 242 days.

McClintock did not hesitate to plunge right back into the Arctic. Once again he took his vessel north in Baffin Bay, but this season he was a couple of months earlier than the year before and managed to cross to the "north water" without any trouble. Ice was very heavy in Lancaster Sound and it was mid-August before the *Fox* arrived at the head of Peel Sound. McClintock hoped to duplicate Franklin's voyage down this channel, but it was blocked by a solid ice barrier and he had to double back around the top of Somerset Island and go down Prince of Wales Strait, where six years before Bellot Strait had been discovered, leading through Boothia to the west. McClintock planned to use this narrow passage as a doorway to the search area, but the strait was impassable; after six attempts to force his vessel through, McClintock resigned himself to spending the winter at Port Kennedy at the strait's eastern end.

The *Fox* was merely a vehicle for getting the searchers as close as possible to King William Island; the search itself would be conducted by sledges in the early spring. Preparatory to these excursions, McClintock crossed the peninsula to talk to the Inuit he expected to find in the vicinity of the magnetic pole. These people possessed a variety of relics from the missing expedition, including spoons, buttons, and knives, and related how a ship had been crushed in the ice in Victoria Strait but all the sailors had reached safety. This meant that one ship would still be visible, and McClintock had high hopes of finding it.

On April 2, 1859, sledges left the *Fox* for King William Island. One party, led by Lieutenant W. R. Hobson, travelled down the west coast of the island toward the very spot where the tragedy was assumed to have taken place while another, led by McClintock, searched the east coast. On his way to the estuary of the Back River, McClintock encountered a camp of Inuit who told him they had visited a wrecked ship on the other side of the island but that it was all but destroyed by repeated pillaging. An elderly woman described fugitives from the *Erebus* and the *Terror* dropping in their tracks as they tried to reach the mainland.

Continuing on his way, McClintock reached the mainland and travelled south to Montreal Island. He searched the island thoroughly, then turned back towards King William Island, heading west along its southern shore. Now he was retracing the path followed by the Franklin survivors, and it was not long before he found ghastly evidence of their fate. A skeleton lay on the beach, half-buried in the snow, the tatters of a blue navy uniform hanging off its bones. "The skeleton—now perfectly bleached—was lying upon its face," recorded McClintock, "the limbs and smaller bones either dissevered or gnawed away by small animals."

Farther along the coast McClintock came upon a newly built stone cairn. Inside was a message from Lieutenant Hobson, dated six days earlier, saying that this spot was as far as he had travelled. He had not seen any sign of a ship but he had found something far more important, the only message left by the Franklin expedition. It was an ordinary piece of naval record paper. On it, two messages were written. The first, dated May 28, 1847, gave a very condensed account of the expedition to that date. As yet there was still hope of working out of the ice that summer and the note ended, "All well." However, in the margins a second message was scribbled which told an entirely different story. Dated eleven months after the first, it briefly stated that twenty-four men, including Franklin, were dead, that the ships had been abandoned and the survivors were heading for the Back River. "A sad tale was never told in fewer words," McClintock truthfully remarked.

This was not the last trace of the expedition to be found. Farther along the coast of King William Island, McClintock came upon an abandoned boat with two skeletons lying inside. Franklin's men had taken boats with them to ascend the Back River after break-up. As long as the way was still frozen, they had used them to carry their supplies and provisions. McClintock found an odd assortment of relics, ranging from the useful—like extra clothing, guns, and tools—to the absurd—like silk handkerchiefs, tooth brushes, and monogrammed silverware. Taken together, McClintock judged it "a mere accumulation of dead weight, but slightly useful, and very likely to break down the strength of the sledge-crews." And this was only a small portion of what the fugitives had taken from their ships. At Victory Point, where they first touched land after crossing Victoria Strait, to lighten their way they cast aside a huge pile of clothing, hardware, and scientific equipment, later found by McClintock and Hobson.

Having cleared up the Franklin mystery at last, the sledges from the *Fox* returned to their ship in mid-June. All that remained was to get safely back to England with the news. And as John Ross had shown a quarter of a century earlier, Prince Regent Inlet could be a difficult place to escape. But August brought open water and the *Fox* sailed home, bringing to an end an astonishing era in the history of northern exploration.

8

Search
for the Pole

Arctic explorers of the nineteenth century and earlier are often compared to the astronauts of our own era, venturing at great personal risk into the unknown, capturing the imagination of an attentive public. One difference, however, is that while space exploration, because of its expense, requires the vast resources of wealthy nation-states, arctic exploration still had room for the freelancer, the eccentric, the individual obsessed by a theory or bitten by the wanderlust; in a word, the amateur.

Charles Francis Hall was one of these amateurs. With little formal schooling, no experience of northern exploration, no personal wealth, and no contacts among the small group of wealthy businessmen who financed the American arctic effort, Hall was an unlikely figure to share the spotlight with Franklin, Hearne, Ross, and the others. But what he lacked in knowledge and background he made up for in enthusiasm and

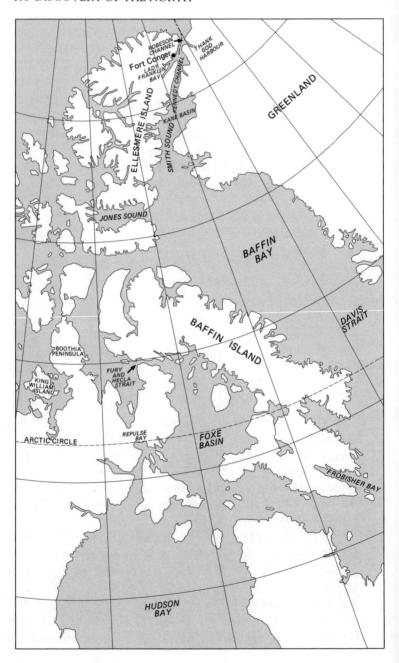

a single-minded determination which bordered on obsession. Hall found in the Canadian North a mission, an outlet for his ambition, an escape from the mundane realities of his life, a spiritual homeland. "The Arctic Region is my home," he announced as he set off on his final expedition. "I love it dearly, its storms, its winds, its glaciers, its icebergs; and when I am there among them, it seems as if I were in an earthly heaven or a heavenly earth." No professional explorer would ever have thought of comparing the Arctic to paradise.

Hall was in his mid-thirties, living in Cincinnati, when he became interested in the Arctic. A qualified blacksmith and engraver, by 1858 he was publishing his own newspaper, an idiosyncratic mixture of news and feature articles about his various enthusiasms. He was a man who became totally preoccupied with a subject to the neglect of almost everything else, and this is what happened when he heard about the missing Franklin expedition. After reading everything he could lay his hands on, and digesting the results of the different rescue attempts, he concluded that survivors of the expedition were still alive among the Inuit, who probably had rescued them and knew of their whereabouts. It was a matter of convincing the natives to tell what they knew.

Several expeditions had already searched the North and questioned the Inuit. What made Hall, a complete novice, believe he could succeed where they had failed? It is hard to know how seriously Hall took his plan and how much he was simply looking for an alternative to the responsibilities of a growing family and a lacklustre career. He himself hinted at divine intervention, claiming that he was "called" to the task and given the job of finding the missing sailors. "My convictions are strong and I could not resist the desire upon me." In 1859 he sold his newspaper and early the next year travelled east to muster support for an expedition.

Americans had only recently become involved in arctic exploration. Ten years earlier Lady Franklin had requested American help in the search for her husband, and a wealthy New York merchant fleet owner, Henry Grinnell, had responded by offering to provide a pair of ships if the navy would man and provision them. The result was the first of two Grinnell Expeditions, neither of which contributed much to the Franklin search, though the second, led by Elisha Kent Kane, pioneered the exploration of the channels and bays separating Ellesmere Island and Greenland, a passage which would be used in the years ahead as the American pathway to the Pole.

These expeditions established Grinnell as the godfather of the American arctic effort and he took Hall under his wing when the printer arrived from Cincinnati. Everywhere, Hall found agreement with his theory that some of Franklin's men were still alive. By May 1860 he had completed his arrangements. He gave his venture a grandiose title, the New Franklin Research Expedition, but all it really amounted to was himself, his supplies, and an 8.5 m, cedar-planked open boat, all of which he arranged to have carried north aboard the whaling vessel *George Henry*. His plan was to acquire an Inuit crew at Baffin Island to take his boat through Frobisher "Strait" (it was still not known that this body of water was closed at one end) to Foxe Basin and on westward to King William Island, making contact with different Inuit groups along the way. Where several experienced, knowledgeable, well-supplied northern navigators had failed, Hall hoped to succeed simply by relying on local natives and his own determination.

The *George Henry* dropped anchor on the coast of Baffin Island near the mouth of Frobisher Bay early in August, 1860. Crossing a narrow neck of land which separated the anchorage from the bay, Hall viewed for the first time the route he hoped would carry him into the heart of the Arctic. As he traced the far shore with his telescope, he was disappointed to find that "it seemed to me that the mountains in that direction united with the land on which I stood, and if so, no 'strait' existed." A few days later some local Inuit confirmed that this was indeed the case, ending at last the three-centuries-old hope that Frobisher Bay was the entrance to a Northwest Passage. Hall was undaunted by his discovery; it made his excursion more difficult but not impossible. Much more serious, however, was the loss of his boat, which was torn free of its moorings and dashed to pieces on the rocks during a furious gale late in September. Without this craft, Hall had no way of transporting an exploring party toward King William Island. Although he did not know it at the time, this mishap marked the end of any hope of pursuing his search for Franklin survivors.

Though his plans were still-born, Hall remained at Baffin Island for almost another two years, living among the Inuit whenever he could and exploring the shores of Frobisher Bay. In a sense, he apprenticed himself to the Inuit way of life in preparation for future expeditions. He travelled with them on hunting parties, shared their meals of hot seal blood and seaweed boiled in salt water, learned their language and listened to their tales and legends. Hall's teachers were a married couple, Ebierbing and Tookoolito, known to the whalers as Joe and Hannah. During the previous decade these two had travelled to England, where they lived for two years, picking up some English and a rudimentary understanding of the alien culture which was responsible for sending ships to their island. When Hall left Baffin to return to the United States, Ebierbing and Tookoolito went with him, and the trio were virtually inseparable until the explorer's death.

Hall was unstinting in his admiration of the Inuit character. He found them hospitable, generous, honest, and wonderfully content. However, as a devout Christian, he could not accept their religious practices as anything other than superstition, and he feared that contact with whalers was "corrupting" the Inuit. To counteract the effects of "reckless white men," and to promote true religion among the natives, Hall had the idea of bringing selected Inuit, like Ebierbing and Tookoolito, to the United States, where they could be instructed in Christianity and civilized manners, then returned to the North as part of a missionary effort to convert the native people. "The Es-quimaux really deserve the attention of the philanthropist and Christian," Hall wrote. "Plant among them a colony of men and women having right-minded principles and, after some patient toil, glorious fruits must follow."

As Hall talked with the Inuit, he kept hearing stories about some white men who many years before had built a sailing ship on the shores of Frobisher Bay. At first he thought these tales were fanciful, but soon he connected them to what he knew about Martin Frobisher's voyages in the 1570s and realized that he was hearing remarkably accurate oral accounts of events that had taken place three hundred years earlier. The Inuit led Hall to islands in the bay where Frobisher and his men had mined their "gold" and built a small house, and the explorer collected a variety of relics which he carried back to the United States. More exciting for Hall than the verification of Frobisher's voyages was the survival of stories about them among the Inuit after the passage of so many years.

I thought to myself, if such facts concerning an expedition which had been made nearly three hundred years ago can be preserved by the natives, and evidence of those facts obtained, what may not be gleaned of Sir John Franklin's Expedition of only sixteen years ago?...I was now convinced, more than I had ever been, that the whole mystery of their fate could have been, and may yet be easily determined with even the smallest well-directed aid. At all events, I felt that, while life and health should be spared me, I would devote myself to this undertaking.

Back in the United States, Hall threw himself into preparing a book about his experiences and organizing another expedition to King William Island. Money was a problem. Hall had little himself, and the American Civil War was preoccupying everyone to the exclusion of arctic adventures. To raise funds, Hall gave public lectures about the Arctic, exhibiting Ebierbing and Tookoolito and their infant son, dressed in sealskin clothing and displaying various native implements.

At one of his talks, Hall met the forty-five-year-old English writer-explorer William Parker Snow, a veteran of the British effort in search of Franklin. Snow was then working in New York as a hack journalist and editor, and, praising Hall lavishly, he persuaded the explorer to hire him to edit and polish the journals Hall had kept at Baffin Island. For a time the two men got along well, but increasingly Hall was irritated by Snow's lack of effort and in the end did most of the work on the book himself, publishing it as *Arctic Researches and Life Among the Esquimaux* in 1864. Snow meanwhile launched an attack on Hall in a New York newspaper, criticizing his lack of scientific training and suggesting that he lied about his Frobisher Bay exploits. Snow carried his feud as far as the courts, suing Hall for money he said was owed to him for editorial work. The case was quickly dismissed—it turned out that Hall was the one actually owed money—but the Englishman continued to berate the American in angry letters to the press.

On July 1, 1864, Hall left this unpleasant controversy behind when he sailed for Hudson Bay aboard the whaleship *Monticello* with his Inuit companions, Ebierbing and Tookoolito and son. He had been unable to get backing for a large-scale expedition and once again was reduced to hitching a ride to the North, where he planned to find some Inuit guides and work his way overland to King William Island. Hall's second expedition lasted five years. For the whole of it he was plagued by uncooperative Inuit, poor health, the interference of whalers, and the difficulties of overland travel on the Arctic coast. Once again he was encouraged by stories the local people told of white strangers appearing on the coast, but the details and chronology were confused, and Hall may have been misled into taking too literally stories which referred to several different visits by several different explorers.

The whalers dropped Hall and his companions in the northwest corner of Hudson Bay well short of his intended winter camp at Repulse Bay, a mistake that cost him a year's travel time right at the start. Early spring, before the snow and ice began to melt, was the only season suitable for travelling on foot and by dogsled in the North. A brief delay for whatever reason could set an expedition back an entire year. That winter Hall spent a month at Depot Island, where the whaling ships passed the frozen months in a sheltered harbour. Whalers depended for their survival on local Inuit, who provided them with fresh meat and winter clothing, but Hall hoped to persuade them not to engage the natives as hunters and instead leave the Inuit free to go with him. The captains predictably were not interested in Hall's needs, and without native guides or transport he was unable to proceed with his plans to reach King William Island.

The story of Hall's continuing frustrations is agonizing to read. One year the Inuit would not proceed across the Pelly Bay area because of hostility with the natives living there; the next year Hall was too sick to travel; the next year he was diverted on a wild-goose chase in another direction by stories of Franklin survivors near Fury and Hecla Strait. The frustration and disappointment took their toll on Hall. He was a combative man at the best of times, easily driven to anger and not always able to command the loyalty of associates. In the summer of 1867, Hall hired five men from the whaling ships to live with him for a year and assist his expedition. The following summer, during an argument, Hall took a revolver and shot one of the men, who he later claimed was leading a mutiny against him. Hall did all he could to nurse him back to health, but after two weeks the wounded man died. The evidence of witnesses tends to contradict Hall's claim of self-defence. It seems more likely that at a time of nervous strain, depression, and keen disappointment he over-reacted to a simple case of insubordination. At any rate, the explorer was never held legally responsible for the discreditable affair; the North was basically a no man's land where government jurisdiction was very unclear.

Finally, in the spring of 1869, Hall succeeded in reaching King William Island. After all the effort and frustration, the accomplishment of his objective was an anti-climax. Rushed for time, he succeeded in collecting a few relics and oral accounts from the local people, but he was unable to discover any documents or other records. Certainly he turned up no survivors and no evidence that any existed. After wandering disconsolately along the beach for a week, he returned to his camp at Repulse Bay and in August boarded an American whaling vessel bound for home.

The indefatigable Lady Franklin was not discouraged at Hall's failure to learn anything definite about her missing husband. Travelling to America, she ran Hall to ground in Cincinnati, where he was paying an infrequent visit to his wife and children. (During the dozen years between 1860 and his death in 1871, Hall spent approximately six months with his family.) But persuasive as she was in her attempt to interest Hall in yet another expedition to King William Island, Lady Franklin could not deflect him from his latest enthusiasm, the discovery of the North Pole. "Having now completed my Arctic Collegiate education," he wrote, blithely dismissing seven years of failure and frustration, "I feel to spend my life in extending our knowledge of the earth up to that spot which is directly under Polaris—the crowning jewel of the Arctic dome." Gone was the religious mission to rescue survivors of the Franklin disaster. Now Hall was motivated by an even nobler calling, unravelling the mysteries of the very Earth itself. "I, for one, hang my head in shame when I think how many thousands of years ago it was that God gave to man this beautiful world—*the whole of it*—to subdue, and yet that part of it that must be most interesting and glorious—at least so to me—remains as unknown to us as though it had never been created."

With the Civil War ended, the government of the United States was open to exotic ventures. Hall spent several months lobbying aggressively in Washington, and was rewarded in July 1870 with a grant of fifty thousand dollars and command of an official naval expedition to the "Arctic regions." The 350-tonne steam tub *Periwinkle* was virtually rebuilt for the trip, adding an outer skin of oak planks 150 mm thick, heavy timbers inside, and an iron sheath covering the bow. The screw propeller was made retractable to protect it from the ice, and the vessel was rigged as a topsail schooner. It was given a new name, too—*Polaris*, North Star, chosen by Hall to indicate his destination. The ship, which steamed away from New London, Connecticut, in July 1871, was commanded by Hall's old crony Sydney Buddington. A twenty-year veteran of the whaling grounds, George Tyson, went along as navigator and a three-man scientific staff was headed by twenty-four-year-old

Dr. Emil Bessels. The complement was rounded out by a crew of nineteen officers and men and eight Inuit, among them the ever-loyal Ebierbing and Tookoolito.

It was accepted by American navigators that the best approach to the Pole was through Smith Sound and the channels beyond, the route opened by Elisha Kent Kane in the 1850s and later followed by Isaac Hayes, two fervent believers in the existence of an "open polar sea." Hall at first thought to follow a variant of this route up the unexplored Jones Sound, but ice conditions convinced him to keep to the more familiar path.

And he was lucky that he did so. The summer of 1871 was remarkably open in northern waters. The narrow passage between Ellesmere Island and Greenland was usually choked with ice, but Hall encountered only clear water as far as the eye could see as the *Polaris* steamed speedily across Kane Basin and into the bottleneck of Kennedy Channel, a point his predecessors, Kane and Hayes, had reached only after days of laborious sledging. Intent on exploiting his good fortune, Hall pressed ahead through Kennedy Channel into another narrow, high-walled strait, which he named Robeson Channel after the American secretary of the navy. At last, on August 30, Hall's rapid progress was halted. At the top of Robeson Channel, as it emerged from the shadow of the last land masses between it and the Pole, the *Polaris* came up against an impenetrable mass of ice, the southern edge of the permanent polar ice cap. Here, after an incredible run of 480 km in just three days, the Arctic turned its other face to the expedition, unleashing fog, snow squalls, and currents that drove the vessel back down Robeson Channel, almost crushing it in the ice. The *Polaris* drifted helplessly for several days before Captain Buddington managed to slip her into a sheltered bay on the coast of Greenland, christened Thank God Harbour, the expedition's home for the approaching winter.

Despite the success of its first season of navigation, the expedition was riven from the very beginning by an atmosphere of sullen mutiny among its members. Later testimony suggests that Buddington, and perhaps not only he, was frequently drunk on alcohol pilfered from the supply brought along by Dr. Bessels to preserve scientific specimens. Worse was the simmering disagreement between Hall and the scientific staff over the objectives of the expedition. Bessels was German, as were his meteorologist and several members of the ship's crew, and according to George Tyson this faction conspired against Hall and his plans to reach the Pole. "There are two parties already, if not three, aboard," Tyson wrote in his journal, as the *Polaris* steamed north. "All the foreigners hang together and expressions are freely made that Hall shall not get any credit out of this expedition. Already some have made up their minds how far they will go, and when they will get home—queer sort of explorers these!"

As long as Hall was alive he managed to paper over the differences. At Thank God Harbour the ship was made ready for winter, and early in October Hall took a dogsled north across Greenland to scout out the route he intended following in the spring. It was on his return from this trip that he suffered what at first seemed like a stroke after drinking a cup of coffee. Following a week in bed, Hall seemed to be recovering, when he suffered a relapse, slipped into a coma, and died. His body, placed in a rude pine box, was buried in a shallow grave excavated with crowbars and pickaxes in the frozen ground and covered with rocks, gravel, and snow.

With Hall's death, Buddington, technically, was in charge, but he lacked the resolution necessary to dominate the men. Without a rigorous discipline the sailors kept to their quarters, falling into a lethargic boredom which was unhealthy both physically and psychologically. Officers and crew feuded among themselves and, adding a macabre note, the ship's carpenter suffered bouts of mental illness, during which he would accuse his shipmates of plotting to murder him in his sleep and would scuttle furtively around the decks like a terrified animal. Excessive though it was, his paranoia was symptomatic of the discord that troubled the expedition from the beginning.

This strained, unhappy atmosphere was not relieved until the following August (1872), when the *Polaris* finally broke free of its winter harbour. There was no enthusiasm left for continuing the assault on the Pole, and Buddington turned the vessel toward the south and home. But almost immediately it was caught in the moving ice floes. Powerless, the *Polaris* drifted south with the current, pumps working constantly to keep the leaking vessel afloat.

On the evening of October 15, in the midst of a howling snowstorm, the ice began to tighten around the hull and the engineer reported frantically that water was filling the hold. It was common practice in the Arctic to keep necessary provisions and equipment on deck when a ship was in peril, so that they could be cast onto the ice if the vessel had to be abandoned. The crew of the *Polaris* immediately began heaving these bundles over the side, while a party on the ice pulled them away to a safe distance. For several hours the men worked feverishly, as giant icebergs driven by the storm smashed the nearby ice floes and high winds and heavy snow made it impossible to see beyond a few metres. Suddenly, at about midnight, the ice, which had been threatening to overwhelm the *Polaris*, broke up and fell away, and the ship, miraculously free, drifted away in the storm. Within minutes it disappeared into the black, snowswept night, leaving a disbelieving group of nineteen people adrift on the ice.

What followed is one of the most amazing survival stories in the history of exploration. For six months, through an entire arctic winter, these nineteen lived on a piece of ice which at times shrank to a size no larger than a suburban backyard. Ten of the nineteen were European or American seamen; the other nine were Inuit men, women, and children. Without the Inuit the sailors would unquestionably have starved to death. The Inuit, chiefly Ebierbing, built snow shelters, hunted seal, cared for the few sled dogs that had been stranded with them, and showed the others how to use the oil lamps so necessary to their existence. And at the very last, as the starving, dispirited survivors could not seem to attract the attention of their rescuers, it was an Inuk who set off in his kayak to bring help.

When George Tyson first found himself and his eighteen companions cut off from the *Polaris*, his immediate thoughts were only of surviving the night and returning to the ship when daylight came. Two boats were on the ice, and Tyson planned to use them to transport the party to shore, where the ship could easily locate them. However, all attempts to cross the ice-choked water to the Greenland shore failed. At one point the *Polaris* appeared briefly in the distance, smoke puffing from its stack, but it disappeared beyond an island and the castaways never saw it again. In fact, the *Polaris* was badly damaged and within a few hours was driven aground and wrecked. The fourteen seamen on board spent the winter camped near the wreck, supplied with food by local Inuit, and in the spring they managed to travel to safety in two boats they manufactured from the remains of the ship.

Meanwhile, out on the ice, the other members of the expedition were forced to admit that rescue was unlikely, and they settled into a small nest of interlocking igloos constructed by the Inuit. The piece of ice they were on was large and not in any danger of breaking up, so at least for the deepest part of winter the camp had an air of permanence about it. The rivalries that had disrupted the *Polaris* were duplicated on the ice, where George Tyson was nominally in charge but admitted he could exercise no control over the seamen, most of whom were German. They lived apart in their own igloo and recognized their own leader, the meteorologist Frederick Meyer. Tyson preferred to live with Ebierbing and Tookoolito and their family, where, ironically, English was spoken; the sailors spoke mainly German. Throughout the ordeal Meyer and his fellows threatened to take a boat, even when the castaways had only one boat left, and head across the ice for Greenland, a mad plan according to Tyson, who nonetheless had no way of stopping them. As it turned out, the attempt was never made and the party remained united.

As the sun disappeared and the temperature dropped toward −40°C, food was the constant preoccupation. The castaways had been left with a dozen bags of biscuit, 285 kg of beef pemmican, fourteen hams, ten dozen small cans of meat and soup, a large can of dried apples, and 9 kg of a chocolate and sugar mix. These supplies were not adequate to feed nineteen people until the spring. Tyson kept the daily allowance at a minimum and hoped to supplement their diet with seal. But it was late fall and winter, and animals of any kind were very scarce. At first the Inuit hunted for seal at breathing holes in the ice; once permanent darkness fell, however, it was difficult to find the holes, even if any animals were about. One by one the sled dogs were slaughtered and eaten, but they were so skinny that they produced little enough meat. By the end of the year daily rations were down to 170 g of biscuit and 280 g of meat per person, washed down with a ghastly concoction called "pemmican tea," a piece of biscuit crumbled into a tin of lukewarm, brackish water along with some powdered pemmican. "It reminds me very much of greasy dish-water," George Tyson wrote. At desperate moments the hungry gnawed on pieces of raw, unshaven sealskin or cleaned the charred blubber residue out of the seal-oil lamps.

The sailors quickly were reduced to listless skeletons. They spent most of their time lying dumbly in their igloos, playing cards, while the Inuit did all the hunting. When they walked, their legs trembled, and physical activity only made the hunger pangs sharper anyway. The boredom was excruciating. There was nothing to read. Even if they had had the strength, it soon was too cold to venture outside. As a result, they fell into a dull stupor, dreaming of food and home. "While the stomach is gnawing," Tyson explained, "and its empty sides grinding together with hunger, it is almost impossible to fix the mind clearly, for any length of time, upon anything else." Cannibalism was a possibility not spoken out loud but never far from anyone's mind.

From time to time the Inuit, usually Ebierbing, managed to bag a seal and it was divided into equal portions, not a piece of which was wasted.

First the "blanket" is taken off [explained Tyson]; that is, the skin, which includes the blubber...; then it is opened carefully, in such a way as to prevent the blood being lost; it is placed in such a position that the blood will run into the internal cavity; that is then carefully scooped out, and either saved for the future use or passed round for each to drink a portion. The liver and heart are considered delicacies, and are divided as equally as may be, so that all get a piece. The brain, too, is a tidbit, and that is either reserved or divided. The eyes are given to the youngest child. Then the flesh is cut up into equal portions. . . . The entrails are usually scraped, and allowed to freeze, and are afterward eaten.

Winter passed agonizingly slowly. It was as if time itself was frozen. Starving, feeble, the nineteen drifted across Baffin Bay, down Davis Strait, and out into the North Atlantic. Ironically, as the weather grew warmer and the castaways moved closer and closer to the busy sea lanes, frequented by sealing and whaling ships, where they were bound to be rescued, their situation grew more and more perilous. As long as the ice held together in a large frozen piece they were relatively safe, but as the giant floes thawed and rotted and broke apart their ice raft grew increasingly smaller and, as Tyson wrote, "the water, like a hungry beast, creeps nearer." In fact, the castaways were in constant danger of being drowned in the frigid water during the last six weeks of their drift.

On March 12, the floe Tyson and the others had inhabited all winter shattered during a gale, and they found themselves on an ice piece measuring just sixty-eight metres by ninety metres, and getting smaller. As the weather remained heavy, this piece crashed and rubbed against others, and its edges dissolved and shattered. By the first of April it was too small to provide a safe haven any longer. The little band of survivors loaded their boat and paddled across an open channel of water to the main body of ice not far away. Even here, however, they were not secure, as the floe might crack beneath them or its edges might crumble into the sea. On April 7 Tyson wrote in his journal: "At six o'clock this morning, while we were getting a morsel of food, the ice split right under our tent! We were just able to scramble out, but our breakfast went down into the sea."

All belongings were now kept in the boat so that everyone could jump clear of the ice at a moment's notice, but the next day the ice divided right between the boat and the tent, and the two pieces drifted apart. The boat, which was crucial to the party's survival, was retrieved only after some of the men managed to hop across a bridge of small ice cakes, each sinking beneath their weight.

Since early March the worst of the hunger was over as seals had become plentiful, but now starvation again afflicted them. Most of the food supplies had been abandoned or lost in the hurried relocations from floe to floe and, with the ice so unstable, hunting was difficult. Even drinkable water was now scarce, the sea washing over the surface of the floes leaving the meltwater foul and brackish.

On the night of April 20, heavy seas began to break over the small cake of ice on which the party was camped. Every ten minutes, with dreadful regularity, a deluge of seawater swept the ice, carrying off the tent, bedding, equipment, everything that was not stowed in the boat. It was imperative that the boat itself be rescued, and the weakened crew struggled to hold it on the floe. As every fresh wave washed in a torrent across the ice, it threatened to throw the boat off the opposite side. Clinging desperately to the gunwales, drenched by the frozen water, battered by chunks of loose ice, some of them as big as the boat itself, straining for a foothold on the smooth surface, the entire party fought to preserve their only chance at escape. Time and again, after one wave knocked them reeling across the floe, they picked themselves up and hauled the boat back to the outer edge, ready for the next blow. "That was the greatest fight for life we had yet had," recalled Tyson. All night they kept up the contest. Finally daylight returned and the party escaped in the boat to a larger piece of ice.

A week later, drenched, without shelter, surviving on the remains of a polar bear they had managed to shoot, the castaways caught sight of a steamship in the distance, the first sign of other human life since the previous October. However, even at the end, rescue was not that simple. The men clambered up a high piece of ice and fired their guns, but the ship did not appear to see them and steamed away in the opposite direction. The next day another sealing vessel was sighted.

This time the Inuk Hans was dispatched in a kayak to inter-cept the vessel.

Captain Isaac Bartlett, uncle of the famous Newfoundland seaman Bob Bartlett, and commander of the sealer *Tigress*, was on deck that morning when he saw Hans and his kayak emerge from the fog. What was an Inuk doing so far from shore off the coast of Labrador? Following this strange, almost ghostly craft to a nearby floe, Bartlett was further astonished to see a crowd of scrawny, hollow-eyed men, women, and children standing on the ice cheering, no other vessel in sight. As the pathetic survivors were helped on board, their horrible ordeal ended on an absurd note. One of the sealers asked Tyson how long he had been on the ice, and when he told him, another asked incredulously, "And was you on it day and night?" Six months of fear and suffering dissolved in laughter.

Charles Francis Hall's third and last arctic expedition had been sponsored by the U.S. Navy, which naturally enough wanted to know what had gone wrong. Not only had no effective attempt been made to reach the North Pole, but the commander was dead under suspicious circumstances, the ship was destroyed and the entire complement of sailors and officers almost lost. An inquiry was convened as soon as the survivors got back to the United States, and all the old quarrels and rivalries were brought out into the open. Hall was an intelligent, resourceful, lone-wolf arctic traveller; perhaps it was no accident that the only organized, large-scale expedition he ever led began in disunity and ended in disaster.

Obviously the expedition had been marked by indifferent leadership, but there was little the government could do about that. What it could do something about was the more pressing matter of Hall's death. Rumours were circulating that he had been murdered and plenty of suspicions were raised by wit-nesses at the inquiry. Throughout his illness Hall himself had been convinced that someone was poisoning him. At times he asked others to taste his food before he would eat it, and his behaviour shifted wildly from angry accusations against al-most every member of his crew to obsequious apologies for past misconduct, real and imagined. Hall especially picked on the expedition's surgeon, Emil Bessels, who led the scientific staff and who had quarrelled with his commander about the objectives of the mission. However, Hall's own journals and papers had disappeared; in the end, testimony was ambiguous and contradictory. Hall, as he lay on his deathbed, believed that he was being poisoned, but that did not mean that he was. Testimony indicated that Dr. Bessels, the key suspect, was tireless in his concern for, and treatment of, his patient. With little evidence to guide them, the members of the board of inquiry ruled that Hall had died of a stroke, and the case was closed.

Closed that is until August 1968, when Chauncey Loomis, Dr. Frank Paddock, and two others flew north to solve a murder, or, more accurately, to discover whether a murder had been committed. The air of mystery surrounding Hall's death had not dissipated with the passage of time. Chauncey Loomis, who was writing a biography of the explorer, hoped to settle the matter by disinterring the corpse and performing an autopsy.

The small party easily located the gravesite on the stony shores of Thank God Harbour. Removing the debris which covered the coffin, they pried it open and found the body wrapped in a faded American flag. "Frank carefully peeled the flag back from the face," Loomis wrote later. "It was not the face of an individual, but neither was it yet a skull. There were still flesh, a beard, hair on the head, but the eye sockets were empty, the nose was almost gone, and the mouth was pulled into a smile that a few years hence will become the grin of a death's head. The skin, tanned by time and stained by the flag, was tightening on the skull. He was in a strangely beautiful phase in the process of dust returning to dust."

Concerned not to disturb the grave, Dr. Paddock performed the autopsy crouched astride the open coffin, the rotting face of Hall staring sightlessly up at him. Loomis had expected to find the body well preserved by the frigid climate, but the internal organs had almost all dissolved and it was not possible to learn very much about how Hall had died. However, the investigators did take hair and fingernail samples from the corpse; when these were tested later at Toronto's Centre of Forensic Sciences, it was proved that Hall had been poisoned with large amounts of arsenic.

This startling discovery still left Loomis with several possibilities. Arsenic was a common medicine in the nineteenth century. Hall, so paranoid in the last weeks of his life, may have tried to treat himself and overdosed by accident. Or Bessels may have been incompetent and unintentionally overdosed his patient. Or someone else may have slipped the arsenic into Hall's coffee and continued to feed him more of the poison as his condition worsened. Loomis was left to speculate that if Hall was poisoned, it may well have been Bessels, who was nursing the sick explorer around the clock, but the only discoverable motive was rivalry over command of the expedition, and this hardly seems sufficient to explain cold-blooded murder. In the end, the mystery of Hall's death remains unsolved, probably forever.

The final expedition of Charles Francis Hall heralded a new orientation in the objective of northern discovery. By the latter half of the nineteenth century, the quest for the open polar sea or, alternatively, a northern polar continent to match Antarctica in the south, had replaced the search for the Northwest Passage. In the same way that the penetration of the frontiers of space became, in the first instance, a race to be first to land on the moon, so did the broader objective of exploration in the Far North become narrowed to the symbolic race for the North Pole. Despite the near-tragedy of the *Polaris*, the Smith Sound–Kane Basin area remained the most promising access route, and subsequent expeditions continued to use it, striking closer and closer to their goal until finally in 1909 Robert Peary made it—or at least got close; his claim is still a matter of controversy.

For the most part these expeditions were not concerned with the exploration of the Canadian Arctic; their sights were set firmly on the Pole. But in 1875–76 two British sailing ships, under the command of Captain George Nares, wintered at the northeastern tip of Ellesmere Island where sledge teams carried out extensive travels along the northern coasts of both Ellesmere and Greenland, achieving for the moment at least a new record for farthest north.

At the beginning of the next decade, as part of a collaborative research effort among several nations, the United States established a polar station, Fort Conger, at Lady Franklin Bay, where one of the Nares ships had wintered. Led by a cavalry lieutenant, Adolphus Greeley, this twenty-four-man expedition accomplished substantial feats of exploration, penetrating farther north than any previous expeditions. However, it is mainly recalled for the horrible fate that befell it when relief vessels failed for two successive years to reach Fort Conger. Despairing of ever being picked up, Greeley and his men set off in small boats in August 1883 to try to reach safety. They landed on the shores of Ellesmere again in Smith Sound, where they expected to find a cache of provisions but did not. The sad company passed a gruesome winter in a ramshackle stone shelter, gradually starving to death. By the time they were rescued in the spring only seven men were left alive.

Whatever the drama and accomplishments of these British and American expeditions, they were interested primarily in the polar quest, not the investigation of the arctic archipelago. It was therefore left to two Scandinavian explorers to continue the discovery of the Canadian North.

9

The Scandinavians

With the Americans preoccupied with reaching the North Pole, the British no longer interested in arctic exploration, and Canadians not yet in the field, the next initiative in the north came from Scandinavia, an unexpected but nevertheless highly appropriate source of arctic explorers. It was, after all, Viking sailors who had begun to probe the arctic archipelago some nine hundred years earlier. The Scandinavians are a northern people, bred to the treacherous seacoasts and the harsh cold. Utilizing dog sledges and cross-country skis, they developed their own unique, highly successful mode of travel, what has been called the "Scandinavian school of arctic exploration."

It was a small school and not all its members confined themselves to the Canadian North. Fridtjof Nansen, for instance, a Norwegian scientist and diplomat, led the first

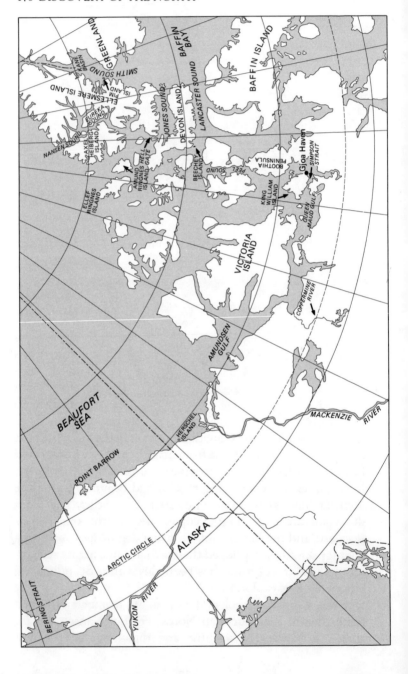

expedition across the Greenland ice sheet, then commanded his specially designed vessel, *Fram*, on a three-year drift across the northern polar basin. The Swedish Baron Adolf Erik Nordenskiöld in 1878–79 became the first person to navigate the Northeast Passage over the top of Russia, and in 1902 his nephew Otto Nordenskjöld accomplished the first important sledge journey in Antarctica. Another Swede, Salomon August Andrée, died in 1897 in a vain attempt to reach the North Pole in a balloon. But along with these great or lesser members, the "Scandinavian school" graduated two Norwegian explorers whose careers flowered in the frozen soil of the Canadian Arctic: Otto Sverdrup, who mapped the remote western side of Ellesmere Island, discovering several unknown islands in the process, and Roald Amundsen, the first mariner to sail a ship through the long-sought Northwest Passage.

Tragedy makes compelling reading. Misadventure, starvation, death, even murder and cannibalism, are the engrossing details of arctic history. However, as a later explorer, Vilhjalmur Stefansson, pointed out, "adventure is a sign of incompetence," and the relative ease with which Sverdrup and Amundsen accomplished their goals should not be allowed to obscure the worth of their contributions.

Their careers are startlingly similar, at least in their early years, before Amundsen went on to eclipse his countryman by reaching the South Pole and becoming one of the most celebrated discoverers of all time. Sverdrup was the elder by eighteen years but he did not become involved in exploration until his mid-thirties, so they seem to be contemporaries. Both men belonged to distinguished, well-to-do families which had made their fortunes from the sea and the land. As youngsters, both mastered cross-country skiing in the Norwegian manner—on heavy wooden boards using a single stick. Both were trained to the sea. As a boy Amundsen spent long hours hanging around the family shipyards and later shipped aboard sealing vessels for two seasons in the ice. Sverdrup spent fourteen years at sea, long enough to earn his master's papers. And both fell under the influence of Nansen, a national hero and the godfather of Norwegian exploration.

It was Nansen who launched Sverdrup on his arctic career, by taking him along on the Greenland crossing and then collaborating with him on the *Fram* expedition. While Amundsen never sailed with Nansen, he, like so many other Norwegians of his generation, was inspired by the older man's example. A seventeen-year-old student at the time, Amundsen was dockside in Oslo that May day in 1889 when Nansen returned triumphantly from the Greenland adventure. "With beating heart I walked that day among the banners and cheers and all the dreams of my boyhood woke to storming life," he later wrote. "And for the first time I heard, in my secret thoughts, the whisper clear and insistent: If *you* could do the North-West Passage!" Four years later Amundsen was back in Oslo watching the *Fram* depart on its dramatic arctic voyage and once again dreaming dreams of polar conquest. Throughout both their lives, Nansen was a revered, almost feared, father figure, the final authority on polar matters whose patronage meant everything, the leader of the "Scandinavian school."

Otto Sverdrup had been back from the polar drift with Nansen only a few days in 1896 when he was given an opportunity to embark on another arctic venture. Three wealthy Norwegians, the philanthropist Axel Heiberg and the brewers Amund and Ellef Ringnes, wanted to finance a scientific expedition. Finding Nansen reluctant to go, they offered the command to Sverdrup, who accepted with enthusiasm. "There are still many white spaces on the map," he explained, "and I was glad of an opportunity to fill some of them with the Norwegian colours." Norway was not yet an independent country; it would remain a province of Sweden until 1905; but nationalist sentiment was running strong, and arctic exploration was a chance to assert Norwegian pride and daring.

Sverdrup received the use of the *Fram* and, after refitting the vessel and choosing a crew, he set sail near the end of June 1898. The purpose of the expedition was to complete the survey of the north coast of Greenland where it was suspected other islands might lie toward the Pole. As it turned out, Sverdrup could not get within five hundred kilometres of his destination. Smith Sound was so choked with huge pieces of ice that the *Fram* sought shelter behind Pim Island, off the coast of Ellesmere Island, and here it remained for the winter, the first of four that Sverdrup and his men would spend on this towering, inscrutable shore.

When one reads Sverdrup's account of his trip to Ellesmere, aptly titled *New Land*, it is easy to forget that he is describing the same harsh conditions that claimed the lives of so many men before him. At times the Norwegians seem to be involved in nothing more arduous than a weekend ski outing. Through forty-eight months in some of the most desolate country on the globe, they never went hungry, surviving comfortably on stocks of musk-ox, seal, hare, and ptarmigan. During the final year, when they were forced by ice conditions to remain for yet another winter in the Arctic, they were so well supplied with food that the only thing they had to give up was their after-dinner cup of coffee. What a contrast to the death march of Franklin's men or the *Polaris* crew eating their moccasins on a drifting iceberg.

Like Edward Parry, Sverdrup recognized the necessity of keeping his men busy as well as healthy during the long polar night. The *Fram* was packed with snow and covered over in the familiar manner, and its interior was made over into a suite of workshops. "There were tents to be made, and sledges to be mended, strengthened, or provided with over-runners; the winter hut, with its 'furniture', and shed for provisions, had to be built and put up, single kayaks altered into double ones, food prepared for the dogs, a forge with its appurtenances made, all the provisions required for the journey weighed and packed—in short, there were innumerable things to be done, and no time to be lost. The *Fram* was simply transformed into a large workshop, where every kind of handicraft and industry was carried on." To keep spirits high the men published a pair of "newspapers" and celebrated holidays with music, singing, and special meals, when they replaced their winter skins with neckties and starched collars. One winter the expedition's zoologist, Edvard Bay, wrote a novel, read avidly by all the company, about some descendants of the ancient Vikings discovered living in a fertile valley in remotest Greenland. In sum, there was none of the dangerous inactivity which led to boredom, illness, and mutiny on other expeditions.

The first winter, Sverdrup still intended to press on to northern Greenland, and all efforts were bent on preparing for the next summer's cruise in that direction. In October the sun disappeared below the horizon; Sverdrup left a memorable description of the sense of isolation, even dread, this sight produced among the men.

> We were looking at the sun for the last time that year. Its pale light lay dying over the inland ice; its disc, light red, was veiled on the horizon; it was like a day in the land of the dead. All light was so hopelessly cold: all life so far away. We stood and watched it until it sank; then everything became so still that it made us shudder—as if the Almighty had deserted us, and shut the gates of Heaven. The light died away across the mountains, and slowly vanished, while over us crept the great shades of the polar night, the night that kills all life.

But the dark months passed easily enough. Toward the end of February the sun returned, signalling the beginning of the sledging season when small excursions were made in several directions to hunt, botanize, and explore. In April, Sverdrup and Bay hiked across the high interior of Ellesmere to the head of a deep fjord on the western side, only the second party to traverse the island. "And on the other side of the fjord was a great chain of mountains, several thousand feet in height, with snow-filled clifts and black abysses, jagged peaks and wild precipices." Sverdrup was looking at the island he would later name Axel Heiberg; he and Bay were the first modern explorers to set eyes on it.

Back at the *Fram* the ice finally relented late in July 1899, and the vessel steamed out into Smith Sound to have another try at penetrating Kane Basin. But, after repeated attempts to batter a path through the heavy ice, Sverdrup once again had to retreat. To return home at this point, with so little accomplished, was unthinkable; so Sverdrup now changed his agenda. Instead of Greenland, circumstances had given him another puzzle to solve. The High Arctic west of Ellesmere was a vast unknown, occasionally glimpsed at a distance but never explored. Before he left Norway, Sverdrup had received permission from his backers to "sail whither I would" if his original goal was for some reason unattainable. He now felt at liberty to take the *Fram* westward into Jones Sound in an attempt to skirt the southern end of Ellesmere and find out what was on the other side.

For the next three years the *Fram* harboured comfortably in the deep fjords of southern Ellesmere. After attempting, and failing, to work the ship up the west coast in the summer of 1900, Sverdrup made winter headquarters in Jones Sound and carried out the actual exploration by dogsled. In three successive springs the Norwegians completed journeys of astounding length and difficulty, all but completing the circumnavigation of Ellesmere, identifying and circling the Ringnes Islands as well as Axel Heiberg, and charting about three hundred thousand square kilometres of new territory.

They did all this by mastering the complementary use of dogs and skis. Dogs had been used as draft animals in the Arctic by the Inuit since before recorded history began, and Edward Parry had pioneered their use by European explorers eighty years before. John Rae, Bedford Pim, and Francis McClintock all used dogs, as did Charles Francis Hall, but none to such great effect as Sverdrup, who appreciated how to manage the animals instead of simply driving them. The Eskimo dog is a fierce, temperamental beast, capable of great speed and endurance but very difficult to control. "Each man has his own team," explained Sverdrup, "which he feeds, thrashes, and defends from the others. He looks after them when they are ill, and receives, in return, their entire and absolute devotion. But to eradicate the wild animal in them is altogether beyond human power." The trick was not to tame them but to turn their ferocity to best advantage, to treat them not as beasts of burden but as companions, with their own needs and limitations. "On journeys like ours, where so much depends on the dogs, relations spring up of such mutual confidence and affection that you come to regard your team as a band of friends."

The use of skis was Sverdrup's peculiar contribution to arctic technique. In Norway cross-country skiing was more than a sport, it was a common mode of transportation. Sverdrup himself had been an excellent skier since he was a boy. On the glaciers of Greenland, he and Nansen already had proven that skis were an effective means of long-distance travel in arctic ice and snow. What Sverdrup did on the Ellesmere expedition was show how a man moving along on skis could accompany hauling dogs and, instead of weighing down the sledge, free up valuable space for provisions and equipment.

Skis and dogs by no means made arctic travel easy. The Norwegians' discoveries were made at great personal risk and effort. For the most part, on their journeys they kept to the sea ice abutting the shoreline, investigating each fjord as they came to it in case it was a strait leading somewhere else. The ice in these channels was often broken by pressure and heaped into towering walls through which a path had to be excavated. Blizzards and fog forced the travellers to remain tent-bound for days on end while ravenous wolf packs threatened the dogs. In late spring, if they stayed out too long, they ran the risk of breaking through the ice in places where brisk currents had weakened the surface from below.

One of the worst trips was up a strait called Hell Gate at the southeast corner of Ellesmere. Sverdrup described it:

The ice was worse than ever and in places was so impracticable as to baffle description. Towering pressure-ridges which had been forced high up against the cliffs in many places compelled us to cut a path, foot by foot, through blocks and hummocks of calf-ice. Then, suddenly, we would be confronted with a fissure so large that the only way of crossing it was to fill it up by shovelling in cart-loads of snow. In other places avalanches had carried boulders, hummocks, and ridges with them into the sea. Where this had happened the snow was as hard as ice, and we had to take to the picks and spades once again. The dogs were unharnessed and we dragged the sledges ourselves across the critical spot. High above hung menacing precipices and cliffs supporting enormous cornices which at any moment might fall, sweeping rocks, men, dogs and sledges with them into the whirling stream below. Here and there a landslip had occurred, carrying away the snow and leaving behind it only black debris, so that we had to clear a way, stone by stone, before we could get our sledges across.

Another time Sverdrup and Ivar Fosheim, returning from a sledge trip, were following a narrow valley back to the *Fram* when suddenly a sheer wall of ice too high to scale halted their progress. The only passage was an arching tunnel formed by the river running through the ice mass. It was either turn back and lose precious days, or enter the tunnel and risk being crushed by the huge blocks of ice which periodically fell from the roof of the passage to the riverbed. Sverdrup and Fosheim decided to risk it.

From the roof hung threateningly above our heads gigantic blocks of ice, seamed and cleft and glittering sinisterly; and all around were icicles like steel-bright spears, and lances piercing downwards on us. Along the walls were grotto after grotto, vault after vault, with pillars and capitals in rows like giants in rank; and over the whole shone a ghost-like bluish-white light which became deeper and gloomier as we went on. It was like fairyland, beautiful and fear-inspiring at the same time...

When they emerged safely at the other end, Sverdrup remarked with characteristic understatement: "It is very wonderful, now and again, to come right under the mighty hand of Nature."

By the summer of 1902, Sverdrup and his men had located and explored Eureka and Nansen sounds, reaching the northwestern extremity of Ellesmere, the last piece of land in that direction before the Pole. As well, they had collected fifty-three large cases of scientific specimens: rocks, plants, animals, and fossils. It was time to go home. In August they managed to work the *Fram* out of its harbour, and late in September they arrived back in Oslo, having added more new arctic territory to the map than any other single expedition to date. Only Sir John Ross had spent as many winters in the ice, and certainly not with the same success.

When Sverdrup brought the *Fram* into Oslo harbour after four years away from home, he probably noticed the hustle and bustle associated with the outfitting of another arctic vessel riding dockside on the swell. The wooden sloop *Gjoa* had arrived in the Norwegian capital that spring from the northern seaport of Tromso, where it had been engaged in the coastal herring fishery for the past three decades. Rescued from this congenial obscurity by its new owner, Roald Amundsen, the *Gjoa* was being prepared for an assault on the Northwest Passage. Compared to the *Fram*, it seemed an unsuitable vessel for northern exploration. It was seaworthy enough, but weighed just 42 tonnes, with only a thirteen-horsepower engine and a crew of six, surely too small, under-powered, and undermanned to withstand the press of arctic ice. But Amundsen was a professional explorer, and his choice of ship, like every other aspect of his expedition (except possibly the finances), showed scrupulous planning and attention to history. He knew that the voyage would take him close to shore through narrow channels littered with shoals and that such waters were best attempted by a light vessel with a shallow draft. Events would prove him correct in this regard, as they would justify his belief that small expeditions living off the land were much more likely to succeed than large ones reliant on imported provisions. John Rae was much more his mentor than John Franklin.

Amundsen had been preparing himself for the Arctic for several years. As a young man he entered medical school at the insistence of his mother, but when she died he abandoned formal education for the practical study of polar exploration. His cross-country ski trips, his sealing voyages, his participation in an expedition to Antarctica, even his jogging and long-distance cycling were all aimed at preparing him for survival in extreme conditions. Despite the fact that he was a novice commander on his first trip into the Canadian Arctic, when the *Gjoa* departed in June 1903, Amundsen was probably more prepared for what lay ahead than any of his predecessors.

In order to attract financial support, Amundsen needed a scientific rationale for his voyage. He found one in the debate current at the time about whether the earth's magnetic poles were stable or movable. James Clark Ross had located the North Magnetic Pole on the coast of Boothia in 1831, but some scientists argued that it had shifted position in the intervening years. Amundsen's task would be to determine the precise location of the pole and compare it to Ross's findings. To this end, he spent several weeks in Germany studying with an expert in terrestrial magnetism, learning to make the necessary calculations and observations. But Amundsen was much more a discoverer than a scientist, and his thoughts were on the Northwest Passage as the *Gjoa* made its way across Baffin Bay and into Lancaster Sound, following the route of so many mariners who had made the attempt and failed. At Beechey Island he paused briefly to survey John Franklin's last winter harbour, then plunged ahead into the unknown.

As the *Gjoa* ran easily down Peel Sound through a thick fog, Amundsen worried that, like Franklin, he would come up against an impenetrable wall of ice that would throw him back and thwart all his plans.

Then, as I walked, I felt something like an irregular lurching motion, and I stopped in surprise. The sea all around was smooth and calm, and, annoyed at myself, I dismissed the nervousness from my mind. I continued my walk and there it was again! A sensation, as though, in stepping out, my foot touched the deck sooner than it should have done, according to my calculation. I leaned over the rail and gazed at the surface of the sea, but it was as calm and smooth as ever. I continued my promenade, but had not gone many steps before the sensation came again, and this time so distinctly that I could not be mistaken; there was a slight irregular motion in the ship.... It was a swell under the boat, a swell—a message from the open sea. The water to the south was open, the impenetrable wall of ice was not there.

However, if the passage was open it still had to be navigated, and Amundsen quickly discovered how perilous a voyage it was going to be. Unlike Franklin, who took his ships to the west of King William Island, where the ice caught them, Amundsen kept to the inside passage between the island and the mainland. While free of heavy ice, this route was studded with small islands and rocky shallows, and twice the *Gjoa* ran aground.

The second time almost ended the expedition. The vessel got firmly lodged on a reef for two days with a howling gale tearing at the rigging and heavy seas smashing the hull against the rocks. The ship was so far hung up that the only way off was forward across the reef to open water on the other side, and in desperation sails were raised to give added push. "The mighty press of sail and the high choppy sea, combined, had the effect of lifting the vessel up," recalled Amundsen, "and pitching her forward again among the rocks, so that we expected every moment to see her planks scattered on the sea." As the battered *Gjoa* seemed to be on the verge of breaking up, the crew hurried to lighten her by tossing the deck cargo overboard; this manoeuvre, combined with a fortuitous gust of wind from astern, at last carried the vessel across the rocks.

On September 12, the *Gjoa* entered its winter harbour on the southeast corner of King William Island, a snug cove well protected from ice and wind, which the members of the expedition christened *Gjoahavn*, Gjoa Haven. The harbour turned out to be located on the path of migrating caribou crossing the freshly frozen strait to the mainland. While the ship was readied for the winter and various makeshift buildings were erected on shore, a few of the men laid in a plentiful stock of fresh meat. As well as food, the caribou provided skins to make winter clothing, if Amundsen and the others could figure out how to treat the hides. Skin garments were far superior to wool. They did not absorb as much moisture, dried easily, remained cleaner, kept out the wind, and felt warm as soon as they were put on. However, it took skill to manufacture them. Luckily for Amundsen, he was saved the trouble by the appearance at the harbour of a group of local Inuit.

Amundsen had read about previous unfriendly encounters between Europeans and Inuit in the Arctic. So when a small party of natives was spotted on the crest of a nearby hill, he went out to meet them armed and suspicious. But instead of hostility, the Inuit greeted the strangers with cries of friendship, and rifles were cast aside as the two groups embraced. The curious natives, who had never seen Europeans before, came to the ship and spent the night. On their next visit they brought dressed caribou skins to barter. A few days later Amundsen visited their camp, six snowhouses several hours from the ship. As they approached, his guides called out.

And immediately the inhabitants of the camp swarmed towards us. It was, indeed, a strange scene; I can still picture it, and shall never forget it. Out in the desolate snow landscape I was surrounded by a crowd of savages yelling and shouting one above the other, staring into my face, grabbing at my clothes, stroking and feeling me. The rays filtered through the ice-windows of the huts, out into the last faint dusky-green shimmer of fading daylight in the west.

In most respects these were stone-age people who produced fire by rubbing sticks together and possessed hardly any metal goods. Yet, unlike other explorers, Amundsen did not allow this lack of western technology to blind him to the generosity and good nature of the Inuit and the valuable lessons they had to teach him about surviving in the North. In fact, after observing these people off and on for two years, Amundsen concluded that his culture had little to offer them.

During the voyage of the *Gjoa* we came into contact with ten different Eskimo tribes in all, and we had good opportunities of observing the influence of civilization on them, as we were able to compare those Eskimos who had come into contact with civilization with those who had not. And I must state it as my firm conviction that the latter, the Eskimo living absolutely isolated from civilization of any kind, are undoubtedly the happiest, healthiest, most honourable and most contented among them. It must, therefore, be the bounden duty of civilized nations who come into contact with the Eskimo, to safeguard them against contaminating influences, and by laws and stringent regulations protect them against the many perils and evils of so called civilization....My sincerest wish for our friends the Nechilli Eskimo is, that civilization may *never* reach them.

In the new year, 1904, the Norwegians began preparing for a spring sledge journey to the magnetic pole, especially learning from one of the Inuit how to construct an igloo. Amundsen believed that tents were only suitable in temperatures above −30°C; beyond that overland travellers had better know how to build a snowhouse or risk freezing to death. Even with his customary thorough preparations, however, Amundsen's first sledge trip was abortive. Departing Gjoahavn on March 1 in −60°C temperatures, too cold even for the dogs, the party had to return after three days. A month later it was a different story. On April 26 Amundsen and Peder Ristvedt, the *Gjoa*'s engineer, reached the spot on Boothia where James Clark Ross had fixed the North Magnetic Pole, to discover that it was no longer there. Even though the two never did locate the new pole, missing it by forty-eight kilometres, their excursion proved the main point, that the magnetic pole was not a fixed point.

The Norwegians spent a second winter at Gjoahavn, perfecting their sledging technique, observing the Inuit, and completing magnetic observations crucial to the scientific objectives of their voyage. By the summer of 1905 this work was done, and on August 13 *Gjoa* left the harbour and resumed its navigation of the Northwest Passage. Immediately, the vessel plunged into Simpson Strait, a treacherous channel never before travelled by ship. In the bow one crewman handled a lead line to test for depth; aloft in the crow's nest another watched anxiously for submerged rocks. "We were in the midst of a most disconcerting chaos," described Amundsen; "sharp stones faced us on every side, low-lying rocks of all shapes, and we bungled through zigzag, as if we were drunk. The lead flew up and down, down and up, and the man at the helm had to pay very close attention and keep his eye on the look-out man who jumped about in the crow's nest like a maniac, throwing his arms about for starboard and port respectively, keeping on the move all the time to watch the track." After four days of this, the *Gjoa* emerged into the slightly safer waters of Queen Maud Gulf, but it was another week before the ship had manoeuvred its way through the last of the narrow straits into Amundsen Gulf, an area well populated with American whalers, who reached the Beaufort Sea from the west via Alaska.

On August 27, Amundsen recalled:

At 8 a.m. my watch was finished and I turned in. When I had been asleep some time, I became conscious of a rushing to and fro on deck. Clearly there was something the matter, and I felt a bit annoyed that they should go on like that for the matter of a bear or a seal. It must be something of that kind, surely. But then Lieutenant Hansen came rushing down into the cabin and called out the ever memorable words: "Vessel in sight, Sir!" He bolted out again immediately, and I was alone.

The Northwest Passage had been accomplished—my dream from childhood. This very moment it was fulfilled. I had a peculiar sensation in my throat; I was somewhat overworked and tired, and I suppose it was weakness on my part, but I could feel tears coming to my eyes.

Amundsen may be forgiven for believing that this encounter with the whaleship *Charles Hanson* marked the completion of his voyage. He was now in familiar waters, with all the unknown dangers behind him. But the Arctic is never predictable. Before the *Gjoa* could get clear of the Beaufort it was trapped by the gathering ice at King Point, just to the west of the Mackenzie River, and forced to spend the winter there. During these long months, Amundsen joined two Inuit and an old whaling captain on an eight-hundred-kilometre overland sled trip from the Arctic coast to Eagle City, Alaska, on the banks of the Yukon River. The Inuit were carrying mail from the whaling fleet harboured at Herschel Island; Amundsen went along because Eagle City was the closest telegraph station, and he wanted to broadcast news of his success as soon as possible. It cost him over $750 to send a cable to Fridtjof Nansen; or rather it cost Nansen, since Amundsen did not have a penny and had to send the telegram collect; but it meant that word of the expedition's triumph reached the outside world long before the *Gjoa* did.

Returning to King Point, Amundsen waited restlessly for the opening of navigation. Finally, in July 1906, the ship got under way and that summer passed around Point Barrow and out of the Arctic, completing the last leg of the Northwest Passage.

The quest that Europeans had begun so many years before was over. The Northwest Passage had been conquered. The Norwegians returned home to be fêted as national celebrities, and Amundsen embarked on a triumphal tour of Europe. His account of the expedition, published in English in 1908, won the respect of critics for its simplicity and understated heroism. To Norwegians the voyage of the *Gjoa* was an affirmation that the old Norse spirit was present still in the newly independent nation. "His voyage in the little *Gjoa*," wrote Axel Heiberg, "is a worthy parallel to the old Norsemen's bold voyages in their small ships to Greenland and Vinland, and a visible proof to the world that the determination which led a Leif Erikson on the first crossing of the Atlantic in history, still lives in the Norwegians of our day."

Yet, however much Amundsen's expedition was a triumph of courage and seamanship, it has to be admitted that it was a bit irrelevant. The existence of the passage had long been known; it was inevitable that someone would someday trace its course. But what was its significance? Transcontinental railways had long since provided a bridge across America, the original motive for arctic discovery. Amundsen's passage, one of several now known to be navigable, has not proved of much economic value. Even today mammoth tankers and icebreakers have not succeeded in making the passage a reliable transportation route. The dream of a Northwest Passage had motivated so many arctic expeditions and cost so many lives and so much suffering. In the end, its accomplishment seems curiously anti-climactic.

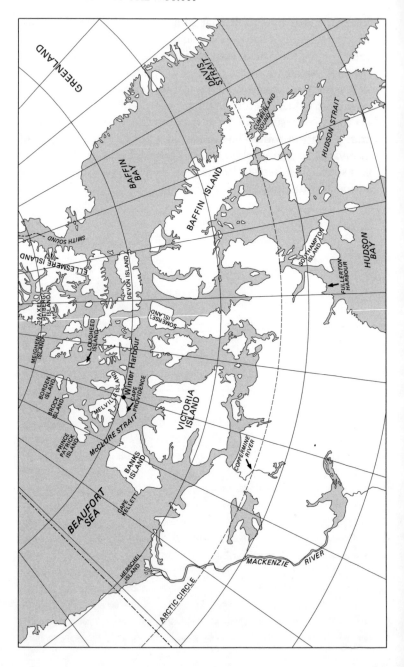

10

Canada Claims
the Arctic

The Arctic in the early twentieth century was no longer a completely isolated frontier. When Roald Amundsen sailed the *Gjoa* through the archipelago, he encountered whalers, traders, explorers, and missionaries from a variety of countries. In the Davis Strait area, whalers from Europe had been active for two hundred years, while at the other end of the archipelago American whalers had been cruising the Beaufort Sea since 1889. Likewise, northern Hudson Bay became a favourite whaling ground after the first American ships wintered there in 1860.

In the wake of the whalers came traders, bartering with the Inuit for exotic items such as musk-ox hides, sealskins, walrus ivory, and fox furs. Soon police and missionaries arrived on the scene, each charged with protecting the Inuit from the excesses of a foreign culture. And, of course, explorers from different countries continued to be active in the North. Otto Sverdrup was just back from his four years on Ellesmere Island; Robert Peary, the American, was penetrating the Smith Sound corridor preparing for his assault on the Pole; and in 1906 a combined Anglo-American expedition arrived in the western Arctic to begin its search for undiscovered land out in the Beaufort Sea.

Despite all this varied activity, the Arctic was essentially unclaimed territory as the new century dawned. Most of the early exploration in the area had been carried out by British seamen and traders, and for this reason, prior to 1870, the archipelago was taken to belong to Great Britain. It was in that year that Rupert's Land, the vast territories of the Hudson's Bay Company which now comprise most of western Canada, was transferred to the young Dominion of Canada. Manitoba was immediately created a province, and the rest of the tract, populated at the time by native groups and the odd trader, was simply designated the North-West Territories and left to await the influx of agricultural settlers later in the century. Ownership of this land was never in doubt, but far to the north the status of the arctic islands remained unclear. Eventually it was decided that they had not been included in the original transfer and in 1880, after much procrastination, Canada took possession of the archipelago as well, primarily to prevent the Americans from staking a claim. As John A. Macdonald warned, "when England had abandoned that country, and Canada was so faint-hearted as not to take possession of it, the Americans would be only too glad of the opportunity, and would hoist the American flag and take possession of the territory."

It was one thing to accept the northland as a gift and quite another to proceed with effective occupation. The government in Ottawa actually had no intention of bothering itself with its newest acquisition. The Arctic was too far away and too sparsely populated. The minister of justice advised that "no steps [will] be taken with the view of legislating for the good government of the country until some influx of population or other circumstance shall occur to make such provision more imperative than it would at present seem to be." It was not until 1895 that the unorganized territories were divided into the districts of Ungava, Yukon, Mackenzie, and Franklin, the latter including the arctic islands. This step signifies the beginning, however half-hearted, of Canadian administration in the Arctic.

As the Canadian West showed signs of becoming a fertile wheat-producing area, attention turned to the Hudson Bay route as a possible transportation link between the interior and the North Atlantic shipping lanes. In the early summer of 1897, Captain William Wakeham sailed from Halifax on the Scottish whaleship *Diana*, leased by the Canadian government to investigate ice and weather conditions in Hudson Strait. The expedition completed six traverses of the strait, proving that the open season extended well into October; as well, it surveyed hundreds of kilometres of coastline on both sides of the passage. More significant from the point of view of sovereignty, Wakeham steamed north to Cumberland Sound, where he landed on Baffin Island at a whaling station, hoisted the Union Jack, and declared "Baffin's Land with all the territories, islands and dependencies adjacent to it" part of Canada. This was the first time any portion of the Arctic was claimed by an official representative of the federal government.

Assembled in a curious crowd around the flagpole as Wakeham read his formal proclamation, 140 Baffin Island Inuit must have speculated uncertainly about what this ceremony forebode for their way of life. These natives were part of a much larger number whose lives were being transformed by the activities of traders and whalers from Great Britain and the United States. Initially whaling had taken place from ships in open water for a brief period each summer, and there had been limited contact between sailors and Inuit in the North. From the middle of the nineteenth century, however, whalers planted shore stations, staffed by one or two outsiders and a workforce of local Inuit, and supplied in the summer by ship. These stations supplemented their haul of whale products by trading furs, skins, and ivory from the natives; indeed, as whale stocks declined, trade in these other items provided most of the profits. By the end of the century the Cumberland Sound area hosted three of these establishments and northern Hudson Bay had one; by the outbreak of World War I several others had opened for business.

In the western Arctic, Herschel Island, a small rocky island off the Yukon coast, was the centre of land-based operations. American whalers reached the Beaufort Sea in 1889 and recognized that Herschel offered a safe harbour, conveniently located close to the whaling grounds near the mouth of the Mackenzie River and those farther east and north. After cruising these grounds into early September, the whalers would retreat to Herschel, where as many as fifteen vessels and their crews might pass the winter, frozen in the ice until spring break-up released them to renew the hunt.

The impact on the Inuit of sustained contact with outsiders was profound. On the one hand, they gained access to useful items of technology, such as guns, boats, knives and metal-ware, which improved the productivity of the hunt and the efficiency of domestic activities. On the other hand, the Inuit were hard hit by diseases imported by the whalemen and by the depletion of animal resources on which they had relied for hundreds of years.

Epidemics were the most immediately devastating effect of contact. On Southampton Island in northern Hudson Bay an entire population of Inuit, the Saglermiut people, was wiped out by an infectious disease, possibly typhus, imported on board a Scottish supply ship. And they were just an extreme example of what occurred all across the Arctic. Without natural immunities, the Inuit were easy prey for a host of deadly diseases, including smallpox, pneumonia, scarlet fever, even measles.

Over the longer term, the depletion of animal stocks was just as critical for the Inuit. Whalemen in their winter harbours were hungry for fresh meat, especially caribou, which the natives hunted for them on the mainland. The introduction of firearms made the hunt even more destructive, and huge numbers of animals were slaughtered. Musk-oxen, though not favoured for their meat, were pursued for their hides, and they too began to disappear. The loss of local animal resources caused the Inuit to rely on traders for processed food and for manufactured clothing to replace the caribou skins no longer available.

As well as these visible changes, the arrival of whalers and traders changed traditional Inuit society in subtler ways, by replacing subsistence hunting and fishing with elements of the wage economy. Some natives actually worked for the new-comers for a part of each year as hunters and whalers, and those who did not at least traded with them. Leather clothing was manufactured for sale instead of personal use; fur-bearing animals were harvested as cash crops. Inuit settled in camps around the whaling harbours or trading stations, disrupting their usual seasonal cycle of nomadic subsistence.

The proximity to the outsiders had unfortunate social results. Alcohol was traded, native women were debauched, venereal disease spread. The whalers at Herschel Island were the worst offenders. "Each year a vessel is loaded at and dispatched from San Francisco with supplies for this fleet, of which cargo liquor forms a large share," reported a North-West Mounted Police officer in 1896. "This liquor is sold or traded to the natives for furs, walrus ivory, bone and their young girls who are purchased by the officers of the ships for their own foul purposes." After visiting Herschel in 1905, Roald Amundsen remarked: "That things on board some of these American whalers were not as they ought to be there can be but little doubt; but, having no positive proofs, I prefer not to mention the many and queer tales I heard during my sojourn there."

Reports of starvation and libertinism filtering out of the North were one reason the Canadian government took a renewed interest in the area. Another reason was the habitual question of sovereignty. Whatever they were doing to the Inuit, American whalemen were posing a threat to Canada's claim that it administered the Arctic. Would the United States government use the presence of its whalers as an excuse to raise its flag over the archipelago? "They are south of us for the entire width of our country," warned Senator W. C. Edwards in a letter to the prime minister, Wilfrid Laurier; "they block our natural and best possible outlet to the Atlantic; they skirt us for hundreds of miles on the Pacific and control the entrance to a vast portion of our territory, and the next move if we do not look sharply after our interests, will be to surround us on the North." Laurier was conscious of the threat. With typical caution, he decided to delay any direct assertion of Canada's claim for fear of annoying its powerful neighbour, instead taking steps to "quietly assume jurisdiction in all directions." To this end a two-man detachment of North-West Mounted Police was installed in a sod hut on Herschel Island in 1903, to maintain law and order, to collect customs fees on trade goods imported from the United States, and to control the liquor trade with the Inuit.

At the same time, a more ambitious expedition was launched into the eastern Arctic. A. P. Low, a geologist with the Geological Survey, was given leadership of the expedition and command of a 420-tonne Newfoundland sealing vessel, *Neptune*, with instructions to land a six-man police detachment on the west coast of Hudson Bay. Arriving at Fullerton Harbour to disembark the police, Low found the American whaleship *Era*, the only vessel in Hudson Bay that year. Together the two vessels passed a companionable winter season frozen in the ice. The *Era's* condition bore obvious testimony to the decline of a once profitable industry. According to Low, the fifty-year-old vessel leaked so badly its pumps were at work continuously to keep it afloat. Even so the forecastle was awash and the crew's beds were soaking wet. Rations consisted of salt meat, canned vegetables, and biscuit infested with bugs. No antiscorbutics were issued, and signs of scurvy were evident. "The crew," continued Low, "are all landsmen without any knowledge of the sea"; he listed their qualifications: "a gunsmith, a clerk in a wholesale drug business, an iron moulder, a mechanic, an ex-soldier, a railway brakesman, an Armenian and several non-descripts 'about town'." All this was a far cry from the proud whaleships which formerly cruised the eastern Arctic.

Despite the fact that whaling was declining, Low and Police Superintendent J. D. Moodie had their instructions. Fullerton was declared a port of entry for Hudson Bay, and all vessels were ordered to report there in the future to pay duty on goods intended for sale or barter. The export of musk-ox skins was banned when Moodie realized how many animals were being slaughtered. Whalers would be forced, after years of living outside the law, to acknowledge the authority of the Canadian police. It was more difficult to explain to the local Inuit that they were no longer masters in their own land. Moodie convened a meeting of twenty-five natives at which he served tea and biscuit and tobacco and told them, according to one witness, "that there was a big chief over them all who had many tribes of different colours and how this big chief, who was King Edward VII, had the welfare of all his peoples at heart." This embarrassing scene was reduced to absurdity when Moodie grandly presented each Inuk with a suit of woollen underwear.

In the summer of 1904 the *Neptune* left Hudson Bay to cruise north up Davis Strait to the Baffin Bay whaling grounds. As well as making contact with several Scottish ships and explaining the new customs regulations, Low landed on Ellesmere and North Somerset islands, where he planted the flag and left behind a proclamation claiming the area for Canada. These declarations, unsupported by anything in the way of a permanent Canadian presence, had more legal form than substance but nonetheless served notice that the government was not about to surrender the Arctic territory by default. Having completed his mission, Low returned south.

While the *Neptune* was still at Baffin Island, Prime Minister Laurier served notice that his government would be continuing its patrols in the eastern Arctic. "At the present time there are whalers and fishermen of different nations cruising in those waters," he told the House of Commons in July 1904, "and unless we take active steps to assert...that these lands belong to Canada, we may perhaps find ourselves later on in the face of serious complications." Laurier announced that another vessel was being dispatched to the area under the command of a fifty-two-year-old sea-captain, Joseph Elzéar Bernier.

A native of L'Islet, Quebec, Bernier had first gone to sea on one of his father's ships when he was just a toddler. He had command of his own transatlantic vessel by the time he was seventeen and eventually logged over a hundred ocean voyages to Europe, South America, Africa, and Australia. As a young captain in 1871, Bernier happened to be docked in the Potomac River not far from the yards where the *Polaris* was being fitted for its ill-starred polar voyage. Bernier himself credited this chance encounter with sparking his own interest in polar exploration, and he began to spend his spare time devouring the written accounts of earlier expeditions.

Slowly a plan began to take shape in his imagination, a plan later confirmed by the polar drift of the *Fram* in 1893–96. He decided that a vessel parked in the ice pack north of Siberia would be carried by polar currents across the top of the world close to the North Pole. "With perseverance and with brave men, we shall certainly overtake our predecessors and plant our flag on the northernmost point on the globe," Bernier declared. In 1898 he began to champion his bold theory in speeches and meetings across the country in an attempt to raise money. For a time early in 1904 it appeared Bernier's dream would come true. The government finally agreed to purchase a ship and ready it for the Canadian Polar Expedition. Late in the summer, however, as Bernier busied himself purchasing food and equipment for a three-year voyage, officials had a change of mind and reassigned the *Arctic* and its captain to the eastern Arctic patrol.

Between 1904 and 1911, Bernier and his ship made four voyages into the Arctic. On the first he went along as captain of the vessel, while overall command of the expedition was given to Superintendent Moodie. On the others he was in charge of the entire mission. His responsibilities were varied and involved collecting duties and licence fees from foreign whalers, charting unmarked coastlines, monitoring the activities of traders and fishermen in the North, and annexing to Canada the unclaimed islands that he visited. For the most part Bernier travelled routes well worn by previous explorers. But this did not necessarily make the going any easier. His men experienced the same hardship and took the same risks as discoverers a century earlier.

In the spring of 1909 the *Arctic* was frozen in at Winter Harbour, the snug haven on Melville Island first visited by Edward Parry. Early in April, second officer O. J. Morin left the harbour with fifteen men and three sledges, heading across ice-bound McClure Strait to plant the flag on Banks and Victoria islands. Without dogs the sailors had to haul the heavily laden sledges themselves. The ice was broken and heaped in great hummocks by wind and current. The temperature hovered at –30°C and a gale beat steadily down on them, piling the snow into impassable drifts. "The roughness of the ice and snowdrifts were beyond description," wrote Morin later, "and we often sank down to our necks in the drifts accumulated during the last storm..." Sleds had to be unloaded and supplies ferried across on the backs of the men, most of whom were sent back while Morin and two others pressed ahead, carrying food to last fifteen days.

On April 26, the exhausted trio reached Banks Island, which they claimed for the dominion. They set up a temporary camp, then set off to walk to Victoria Island, intending to explore Banks Island further on their return. In their absence a polar bear invaded the camp, destroying or carrying off almost all the remaining provisions. Their blankets torn to shreds, the fuel for their stove almost gone, with no food but a few dried biscuits, the men hastily cut short their reconnaissance of Banks Island and began a desperate race back across the strait to the ship. Conditions out on the ice were just as bad, and now added to them was the weakening condition of Morin and the others. The last of the fuel was quickly consumed. Without heat they could not rest for long for fear of freezing, yet with only biscuits to eat they could not continue long without flagging. Much of the time they suffered the intense pain of snow-blindness. Always they were thirsty, since there was no heat to melt the snow and eating it was, said Morin, "like trying to put out a fire with oil."

At this point a stroke of miraculous luck probably saved the lives of the three. Right in the middle of McClure Strait they stumbled over an uprooted tree lying on the ice. Using the wood for fuel, they quickly built a fire to warm themselves and melt some water. Rest was now possible. However, they could not linger. There was still no food, no shelter. They were forced to push on and they were soon reduced to their former state of fatigue and near-starvation. As a last resort, Morin burned the wooden sledge to make some water to drink. There was little enough left to haul anyway; only four biscuits remained of their supplies. Then the men made their final effort. Blinded by the snow, half-starved, afraid to stop in case it should be forever, they staggered toward Cape Providence on Melville Island, where the previous fall Bernier had deposited a cache of food in a cairn. Four days after leaving the charred remains of their last sled, the trio reached the cape. They had survived.

Two years before, far to the south in Ottawa, Senator Pascal Poirier had enunciated a novel approach to the question of Arctic sovereignty. In a speech in the Senate, Poirier suggested that the Arctic be cut up into sectors shaped more or less like pieces of a huge pie, with the Pole at the centre. Each nation bordering on the Arctic—Norway, Sweden, the Soviet Union, the United States, and Canada—would possess the lands lying between its northern coastline and the Pole. In the case of Canada, Poirier's theory granted it ownership of the entire archipelago from 141° west longitude, the border with Alaska, to approximately 60° west longitude. Although it was never recognized in law, the so-called sector theory became the basis of Canadian claims in the North for several years. Certainly Bernier endorsed the theory; in fact, he later claimed to have originated the idea himself. Regardless, he was definitely the first person to put it into practice. On July 1, 1909, while still frozen in at Winter Harbour, the captain unveiled a plaque on a hill overlooking the harbour declaring that every island in the archipelago all the way to the Pole belonged to Canada.

In 1911, the eastern Arctic patrol was cancelled. Feeling that symbolic flag-waving had accomplished as much as it could, the federal government was now interested in supporting projects of solid scientific and anthropological worth. Naturally, therefore, when the Geological Survey was approached early in 1913 by a group of American scientists planning an excursion into the western Arctic, it jumped at the chance to get involved, eventually taking over support of the entire project, dubbing it the Canadian Arctic Expedition. Leader of the expedition was Vilhjalmur Stefansson, possibly the most controversial of all the arctic discoverers.

By the twentieth century it was no longer enough for explorers to be skilled northern travellers; they had to be fluent public speakers and authors as well, able to translate their arctic adventures into public acclaim and financial support. Stefansson met the new criteria enthusiastically. His several books chronicling his experiences sold well, and he was much in demand on the lecture circuit. He was as close to being a celebrity as it was possible to be in an age before the television talk-show. However, his publicity-seeking caused jealousy and contempt among his fellow scientists and explorers, who either did not understand this new dimension to the arctic enterprise or envied Stefansson's success at it. In their opinion he was more showman than scientist, an irresponsible braggart who would sacrifice the aims, even the safety, of an expedition for a few more column-inches of print. And it was true that, resourceful as Stefansson was at surviving an arctic winter, as leader of a large and expensive expedition he was off-hand, disorganized, and arrogant. From the beginning the Canadian Arctic Expedition was plagued by jealousy, disorder, and lack of authoritative leadership.

Vilhjalmur Stefansson was born in Arnes, Manitoba, in 1879. His Icelandic parents had moved to the Canadian West four years earlier; however, they relocated to the United States when the boy was just one, and he grew up in a frontier log cabin in Dakota. Stefansson was a kind of "muscular scholar," an uneasy mix of intellectual and adventurer. Though he was kicked out of one university for not attending classes, he pursued his academic career at Harvard, and it was as a graduate student in anthropology that he made his first visit to the northern latitudes, studying the relationship between tooth decay and diet in Iceland. In 1906 he joined the Anglo-American Polar Expedition, which was heading for the Beaufort Sea in search of undiscovered land north of Alaska. Stefansson passed the winter living among the Inuit of the Mackenzie delta, his first exposure to "going native." Though the expedition aborted, the quest for new land along the western edge of the archipelago continued to preoccupy him.

In 1908 Stefansson went back to the western Arctic, this time accompanied by the zoologist Rudolph Anderson, in search of the "blond Eskimoes," a group of Inuit reportedly living on Victoria Island entirely cut off from contact with outsiders. Working his way eastward along the coast from the Mackenzie, Stefansson met up with these light-skinned, fair-haired natives in the spring of 1910 and lived among them for several months. On his return south he roused a storm of controversy worldwide by suggesting that because of their appearance these people, now called the Copper Inuit, might be descendants of Greenland colonists or even the offspring of survivors of the Franklin disaster. Roald Amundsen called this idea "palpable nonsense," and other scientists passed even harsher judgements. Later Stefansson qualified his opinion, but the damage had been done and the feeling began to grow that he was a man who would put publicity values ahead of the truth.

Stefansson's third expedition initially was going to be financed by the New York Museum of Natural History and the National Geographic Society; the explorer approached the Canadian government only for supplementary help. However, one of the results of the expedition would likely be the discovery of new islands, and the government preferred that Americans have no official basis for claiming them. Stefansson shed his American backers and the expedition was reborn under Canadian auspices. The fifteen members were divided into northern and southern parties; the northern party, with Stefansson in command, would look for undiscovered land north in the Beaufort Sea while the southern party carried out scientific work along the Arctic coast. Each group sailed north in June 1913 in its own vessel, intending to rendezvous at a point on the Alaskan coast. But tragedy intervened. As it edged its way across the top of Alaska, the ship carrying the northern party, the *Karluk*, was caught in the ice and carried away in a storm. Stefansson and some others were ashore at the time on a hunting trip, but twenty-eight crew and scientists disappeared with the vessel. It drifted helplessly in a westerly direction for several months until it was crushed near Wrangel Island. Some of the crew reached the island and eventually were saved, but sixteen men perished in what one historian has called "the greatest arctic disaster since the disappearance of the Franklin expedition."

The loss of the *Karluk* caused Stefansson to change his plans. Instead of exploring the far northern islands, he decided to take a sledge out onto the frozen surface of the Beaufort Sea above Alaska and attempt to travel as far north as he was able, looking for undiscovered islands and taking scientific measurements. When he joined the southern party at its Collinson Point headquarters, however, he felt their hostility and suspicion. Led by Stefansson's old partner, Rudolph Anderson, members of the southern party refused to allow their equipment or their talents to be used in what they saw as a publicity-seeking stunt with little scientific value.

And it was not just his own expedition that mistrusted him. Stefansson seemed to make himself unpopular with almost everyone he met. "Seldom have I seen a man for whom there are fewer good words than in the case for VS along this coast," wrote one of the scientists. Stefansson's brash egocentricity rubbed people the wrong way, and so did his intimacy with the local Inuit, a familiarity which offended many whites less able to bridge the cultural gap. One of these was Charles Whittaker, an Anglican missionary angered by Stefansson's criticisms of the church's activities in the North. Whittaker took his revenge by warning the Inuit not to have anything to do with the explorer and claiming in public lectures that Stefansson was morally depraved. "We should care as much about the Salvation of souls as Stefansson cares about the bodies," he thundered.

In the end Stefansson worked out an arrangement with the scientists that as long as he did not interfere with their work, whatever he did on his own initiative was his business. Ignoring government attempts to recall him, Stefansson accomplished an astonishing series of sledge trips across the open sea ice during the next three years. More than once he was given up for dead, only to appear unexpectedly to replenish his supplies before disappearing again out on the ice. On the first expedition, during the spring of 1914, he and two companions were away from land for three months, coming close to starving to death as they took soundings of the Beaufort Sea floor and sought new islands in the icy waste. After rendezvousing with a relief vessel at Cape Kellett on Banks Island and spending the fall and winter of 1914 there, the Stefansson party set off again in 1915. This time they skirted the coast of Prince Patrick Island and, continuing northward, made the first recorded visit to Brock and Borden islands. The next year, 1916, the explorers added Meighen and Lougheed islands to their list of firsts. In total they travelled about thirty-two thousand kilometres by dogsled and discovered the final important pieces of the arctic archipelago.

Stefansson was a tireless promoter of the economic potential of the "Friendly Arctic." After his return from the North in 1918, he embarked on a lecture tour trumpeting his claims that the polar region was an inhabitable, resource-rich territory which Canada should take steps to control and exploit. Attempting to show the way by example, Stefansson launched a reindeer-raising operation on Baffin Island, followed by a plan to exploit musk-ox commercially. Later he even sent a party of four men to occupy Wrangel Island and claim it for Great Britain. The ramifications of this act embroiled Canada in an international dispute with the Soviet Union and the United States, and the fallout from the incident, coupled with continuing antagonism in scientific circles, damaged Stefansson's credibility. After 1924 he was no longer influential in Canada's arctic program.

Confrontation was not official government style in the Arctic. Suspecting that its ownership of the northern parts of

Sir John Franklin, leader of three horrific expeditions which, between them, accounted for more deaths than did all the other expeditions put together. The disappearance of Franklin and his men in the late 1840s gave rise to scores of expeditions as, for fifteen years, hundreds of men searched for traces of the ill-fated Franklin.

£20,000
REWARD

WILL BE GIVEN BY

Her Majesty's Government

TO ANY PARTY OR PARTIES, OF ANY COUNTRY, WHO SHALL RENDER EFFICIENT
ASSISTANCE TO THE CREWS OF THE

DISCOVERY SHIPS

UNDER THE COMMAND OF

SIR JOHN FRANKLIN,

1.—To any Party or Parties who, in the judgment of the
Board of Admiralty, shall discover and effectually relieve the
Crews of Her Majesty's Ships "Erebus" and "Terror," the

£20,000.

OR

2.—To any Party or Parties who, in the judgment of the
Board of Admiralty, shall discover and effectually relieve *any*
of the Crews of Her Majesty's Ships "Erebus" and "Terror,"
or shall convey such intelligence as shall lead to the relief of
such Crews or *any* of them, the Sum of

£10,000.

OR

3.—To any Party or Parties who, in the judgment of the
Board of Admiralty, shall by virtue of his or their efforts first
succeed in ascertaining their fate,

£10,000.

W. A. B. HAMILTON,

Secretary of the Admiralty.

Admiralty, March 1850.

Spurred on by Lady Franklin, the Admiralty offered a substantial reward for
aid to or information about Franklin's missing ships. The reward of £10,000 was
ultimately given to John Rae and his men for ascertaining the fate of the
Franklin expedition, amid much controversy aroused by Rae's disclosure that
the last survivors had resorted to cannibalism.

One of the would-be rescue parties man-hauling supplies and boats around the top of Bathurst Island, during the search for Franklin. Boats were taken on these excursions in case open water was encountered as the season lengthened into spring. This drawing was made by Lieutenant Walter May, an officer aboard one of the search vessels.
PUBLIC ARCHIVES CANADA # C8756

The *Assistance* and the *Pioneer* were two of the ships dispatched to look for Franklin in 1852. They are shown here in winter harbour, snow packed against their sides to provide insulation, their decks covered with canvas. Later, both vessels had to be abandoned in the ice.
PUBLIC ARCHIVES CANADA # C6694

In 1853 the *Phoenix* (left) and the *Breadalbane*, two Franklin search vessels, were crushed in the ice in Lancaster Sound and the *Breadalbane* went to the bottom. In 1980 the wreck was located underwater about two kilometres off the coast of Beechey Island, and since then it has been visited several times by divers.
PUBLIC ARCHIVES CANADA # C227

A. P. Low and the crew of the *Neptune* hoisted the British flag at Cape Herschel, Ellesmere Island, on August 11, 1904, as part of a low-key campaign by the Canadian government to assert its sovereignty in the North.
PUBLIC ARCHIVES CANADA # PA38265

Captain Joseph Elzéar Bernier on the deck of the *Arctic*, his government patrol vessel.

The *Arctic* at Fullerton Harbour in northwestern Hudson Bay, unloading supplies in 1904 for the newly established police post.

Roald Amundsen, the first person to navigate the Northwest Passage, as he looked in 1908 when his book about the voyage was published.

Villijalmur Stefansson's party setting off from the north coast of Alaska, heading out onto the frozen Beaufort Sea in March, 1914, in search of undiscovered islands.
PUBLIC ARCHIVES CANADA # C23659

The RCMP vessel *St. Roch* began cruising the Arctic in 1928. Each winter it would shelter along the coast and act as a base for police patrols. In 1944 it became the first ship to navigate the Northwest Passage in a single season.
PUBLIC ARCHIVES CANADA # PA121409

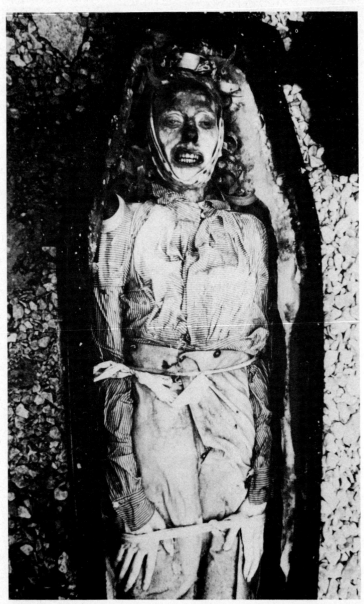

The frozen corpse of John Torrington, a twenty-year-old petty officer on John Franklin's third expedition who died in the spring of 1846 and was buried on Beechey Island. In 1984 his body, preserved in permafrost, was found by scientists investigating the Franklin tragedy. It was concluded that Torrington probably died of pneumonia.
United Press Canada

the archipelago was tenuous, Ottawa preferred to let well enough alone. As long as no other country tried to claim the region, Canada was content with the sector theory and the odd police patrol.

Increasingly, this policy of benign neglect became inadequate. Ever since his return from Ellesmere Island in 1902, Otto Sverdrup had been attempting to persuade the government of Norway to be aggressive about asserting its right to the "New Land." For all that Low and Bernier had raised the Union Jack on Ellesmere, Sverdrup had arrived there first. It was one of the major disappointments of his life that Norwegian officials did not share his enthusiasm for the barren island. Early in the 1920s, however, the Canadian government became concerned that Norway might even yet listen to Sverdrup. With this possibility in mind, the Eastern Arctic Patrol, pioneered by Bernier, was renewed and the RCMP established posts on Baffin, Devon, and Ellesmere islands.

Before the situation with Norway could be cleared up, Canada faced a challenge to its sovereignty from quite another direction, the United States. Anticipating the future importance of polar air travel, the Navy Department of the U.S. was anxious to discover new islands in the northern archipelago where air bases could be built. In 1925 a combined U.S. Navy–National Geographic Society expedition was dispatched to northern Greenland. The expedition consisted of the steamer *Peary*, a support vessel, and three amphibious biplanes. It was led by Lieutenant Commander Richard Byrd, later to become the first person to fly over the North Pole, and the anthropologist-explorer Donald MacMillan. This expedition intended establishing its headquarters at Etah, Greenland, then using bases on Ellesmere and Axel Heiberg islands to launch exploratory flights over the polar sea.

When they heard about the American plans, Canadian officials became alarmed. As far as they were concerned, the flights would be originating in, and passing over, Canadian territory and required Canadian permission. In Parliament the minister of the interior stated categorically "that if foreigners want to go in there they must have permission in the form of a licence." However, Canadian representations were stonewalled by the U.S. government, and the expedition set off without the issue having been resolved.

By previous standards the Canadian response was swift and decisive. Captain Bernier and the *Arctic* were sent to Etah with a government official on board, ostensibly to investigate health conditions among the Inuit and to establish an RCMP post on Ellesmere but also to enforce a new law requiring that scientists and explorers visiting the North be properly licensed. The two expeditions rendezvoused at Etah on August 19, 1925. It is not clear whether the Americans backed down in the face of Canadian assertiveness. They had already encountered delays and poor weather, which had frustrated attempts to establish advance bases, and the planes were not running well. Whatever the exact reason, the Americans departed. The following year, when Donald MacMillan planned another trip to the Arctic, he requested the necessary licence first. Canadian sovereignty had been successfully defended.

Meanwhile, negotiations with Norway began. Chiefly this involved satisfying the claims of Otto Sverdrup who, despairing of his government's timidity, decided that if Norway would not demand Ellesmere he would ask Canada to recompense him for the expenses of his 1898–1902 expedition. Since the explorer had opened up such a huge area of the High Arctic, Ottawa was willing to open negotiations. Late in 1929 an agreement was reached. Canada was unwilling to admit that Norway had a legitimate claim to any arctic territory, but it paid Sverdrup $67,000 on the pretext of buying his charts, maps, and documents. Ironically, fifteen days after the agreement was announced, the old Arctic explorer died.

The settlement with Sverdrup marked the end of a long process by which Canada gained control over its last frontier. It was a process begun reluctantly, at the invitation of Great Britain, and carried on fitfully. When foreign whalers, traders, and explorers forced their hand, Canadian officials reacted with a show of sovereignty. More usually, they preferred a policy of indifference, governing in what one scholar has called "a fit of absence of mind."

In fact, today, fifty-seven years after the agreement with Sverdrup, Canada's control of its arctic territory is still not secure. During the summer of 1985 a U.S. Coast Guard icebreaker, *Polar Sea*, cruised through the Northwest Passage; although the United States informed Canadian authorities of the voyage before it took place, the incident highlighted the refusal of Americans to acknowledge that the passages through the arctic archipelago belong to Canada. As far as the U.S. is concerned these are international waters and its vessels may use them freely. The Canadian government has responded by announcing plans to construct a $450-million icebreaker and has hinted at other steps to ensure that its sovereignty over arctic waters will be as secure as its ownership of the arctic islands.

No one has to convince Canadians today that the Arctic is a valuable territory. Many feel that our hopes for a prosperous future depend on the development of the region's oil and gas potential. The resource wealth of the Arctic has in turn created new problems for the government. In what way should these resources be developed, if at all? If resource exploitation does occur, how should the economic dividends be divided within Canada?

During the discovery period, Indian and Inuit interests were largely ignored by outsiders. Today Native groups are well-organized and asserting their right to a share of the benefits. In a sense an old question is being raised in a new way: who will own the North?

Epilogue

Robert Peary called Vilhjalmur Stefansson "the last of the old school, the old regime of arctic and antarctic explorers, the workers with the dog and the sledge . . ." Stefansson embodied a style of arctic exploration which had been maturing since the pioneering overland treks of John Rae and the first, tentative attempts by British naval explorers to leave their ships and trust their lives to dogs and sledges.

Travelling light, relying at least in part on local food resources and Inuit technology, Stefansson represents the end of an era. There were others who would emulate his style. Several RCMP patrols, for instance, made daring sledge journeys through the archipelago in the 1920s. But, generally speaking, after Stefansson the task of arctic exploration was taken over by motorized technology. Aeroplanes, tractors, skidoos, icebreakers, and even submarines transformed the mode of northern exploration.

Since almost all the northern land masses had been located, discovery was no longer a prime motivation for arctic travellers. Neither was the Northwest Passage, already navigated and found impractical for commercial uses. Increasingly, practical scientific and economic objectives came to preoccupy the arctic project.

The North was now a resource frontier and the great age of exploration inaugurated by Martin Frobisher so many years before was over.

Bibliographic Essay

General

This study is based for the most part on the many journals and memoirs written by the explorers themselves. They will be found below, listed under the appropriate chapter headings. There are several general, secondary sources which I consulted and recommend to anyone wishing to read more deeply in this fascinating subject. Robert McGhee, *Canadian Arctic Prehistory* (Toronto: Van Nostrand Reinhold, 1978) is a handsomely illustrated introduction to the people who inhabited the arctic regions before the first Europeans arrived. An exhaustive chronology of arctic expeditions is in Alan Cooke and Clive Holland, *The Exploration of Northern Canada, 500 to 1920* (Toronto: McClelland & Stewart, 1978). A more concise narrative account, which includes antarctic exploration as well, is found in L. P. Kirwan, *A History of Polar Exploration* (London: Penguin Books, 1959). Leslie Neatby, classics scholar turned enthusiastic student of Canadian arctic history, has written two very readable, authoritative companion volumes about northern exploration: *In Quest of the Northwest Passage* (New York: Crowell, 1958) and *Conquest of the Last Frontier* (Athens, Ohio: Ohio University Press, 1966). Morris Zaslow, ed., *A Century of Canada's Arctic Islands, 1880–1980* (Ottawa: The Royal Society of Canada, 1981) is a collection of articles covering all aspects of northern development in the past century.

Chapter One: The First Voyages

Documents relating to the Frobisher voyages were collected by Vilhjalmur Stefansson in *The Three Voyages of Martin Frobisher*, 2 vols. (London: Argonaut, 1938), and are also reprinted in W. A. Kenyon, *Tokens of Possession: The Northern Voyages of Martin Frobisher* (Toronto: Royal Ontario Museum, 1975). Two books which describe the voyages of the sixteenth and early seventeenth centuries are Tryggvi Oleson, *Early Voyages and Northern Approaches, 1000–1632* (Toronto: Mc-Clelland & Stewart, 1963) and Samuel Eliot Morison, *The European Discovery of America: The Northern Voyages, 500–1600* (New York: Oxford University Press, 1974). Evolving navigation techniques are described in David W. Waters, *The Art of Navigation in England in Elizabethan and Early Stuart Times* (London: Hollis & Carter, 1958), while the European background can be found in: William Foster, *England's Quest for Eastern Trade* (London: A. & C. Black, 1933); James Williamson, *The Age of Drake* (London: A. & C. Black, 1938); and David Beers Quinn, *England and the Discovery of America, 1481–1620* (New York: Alfred Knopf, 1974).

Chapter Two: Seeking the Hudson Bay Passage

The eighteenth-century controversies surrounding the Hudson Bay "passage" are described thoroughly in Glyndwr Williams, *The British Search for the Northwest Passage in the Eighteenth Century* (London: Longmans, 1962). The general background to the Hudson's Bay Company's clash with Arthur Dobbs is in E. E. Rich, *The History of the Hudson's Bay Company, vol. I: 1670–1763* (London: Hudson Bay Record Society, 1958). The Knight expedition is treated in W. Gillies Ross and W. Barr, "Voyages in Northwestern Hudson Bay (1720–1772) and Discovery of the Knight Relics on Marble Island," *Muskox*, no. 11 (1972). Christopher Middleton's voyage is partly the subject of William Barr, "From Wager Bay to the Hebrides: The Duties of an Eighteenth-Century Bomb Vessel," *Muskox*, no. 16 (1975). An excellent biography of Dobbs is Desmond Clarke, *Arthur Dobbs, Esquire, 1689–1765* (London: Bodley Head, 1958).

This is not the place for a complete review of the primary documents. A taste of the controversy can be found in Arthur Dobbs, *An Account of the Countries Adjoining to Hudson's Bay...* (London: J. Robinson, 1744); Christopher Middleton, *A Vindication of the Conduct of Captain Christopher Middleton* (London: J. Robinson, 1743); Henry Ellis, *A Voyage to Hudson's*

Bay by the Dobbs Galley and California in the years 1746 and 1747 (London: Whitridge, 1748); [T. S. Drage], *An Account of a Voyage For the Discovery of a North-West Passage*, 2 vols. (London: Joliffe *et al.*, 1748); E. E. Rich, ed., *James Isham's Observations on Hudson's Bay, 1743* (London: Hudson Bay Record Society, 1949).

Chapter Three: Overland to the Arctic

The best account of Hearne's expedition is his own, edited by Richard Glover, *A Journey from Prince of Wales's Fort in Hudson's Bay to the Northern Ocean, 1769–1772* (Toronto: Macmillan, 1958). Mackenzie's journal is in W. Kaye Lamb, ed., *Journals and Letters of Sir Alexander Mackenzie* (Cambridge: Cambridge University Press, 1970). The introductions in both volumes provide comprehensive overviews and biographies. An exhaustive account of Mackenzie's trip down to the Arctic Ocean is J. K. Stager, "Alexander Mackenzie's Exploration of the Grand River," *Geographical Bulletin*, vol. 7, nos. 3 and 4 (1965).

Chapter Four: The Royal Navy in the North

John Ross's own account of the controversial 1818 expedition is *Voyage of Discovery in His Majesty's Ships Isabella and Alexander for the Purpose of Exploring Baffin's Bay* (London: John Murray, 1819). A supplementary view is available in Alexander Fisher, *Journal of a Voyage of Discovery to the Arctic Regions, 1818* (London: G. Sidney, 1820). Parry recorded his three voyages in William Edward Parry, *Journal of a Voyage for the Discovery of a North-West Passage, 1819–20* (London: John Murray, 1821. Reprinted New York: Greenwood Press, 1968); *Journal of a Second Voyage of Discovery of a North-West Passage from the Atlantic to the Pacific, 1821–23* (London: John Murray, 1824); and *Journal of a Third Voyage for the Discovery of a North-West Passage in 1824–25* (London: John Murray, 1826). John Franklin's two overland expeditions can be followed in his two books, *Narrative of a Journey to the Shores of the Polar Sea, 1819–22* (London: John Murray, 1823. Reprinted Edmonton: Hurtig, 1969) and *Narrative of a Second Expedition to the Shores of the Polar Sea, 1825, 1826 and 1827* (London: John Murray, 1828. Reprinted Edmonton: Hurtig, 1971). Another, partial account of the first expedition has been published by Stuart Houston, ed., *To the Arctic by Canoe, 1819-1821: The Journal and Paintings of Robert Hood* (Montreal: McGill-Queen's University Press, 1974).

Parry's biography is Ann Parry, *Parry of the Arctic* (London: Chatto & Windus, 1963). A less flattering assessment is A. G. E. Jones, "Rear Admiral Sir William Edward Parry: A Different View," *Muskox*, no. 21 (1978). Franklin's two early expeditions are narrated in Paul Nanton, *Arctic Breakthrough* (Toronto: Clarke, Irwin, 1970). Two studies of the British background are Michael Lewis, *The Navy in Transition, 1814-1864* (London: Hodder & Stoughton, 1965) and Christopher Lloyd, *Mr. Barrow of the Admiralty: A Life of Sir John Barrow, 1764-1848* (London: Collins, 1970).

Chapter Five: The Ordeal of John Ross

Commander Ross wrote his own account of the expedition: John Ross, *Narrative of a Second Voyage in Search of a North-West Passage, 1829-1833* (London: Carey & Hart, 1835). A good biography of the elder Ross and his nephew is Ernest S. Dodge, *The Polar Rosses* (London: Faber & Faber, 1973). Back's rescue mission is described in George Back, *Narrative of the Arctic Land Expedition to the Mouth of the Great Fish River, 1833-35* (London: John Murray, 1836. Reprinted Edmonton: Hurtig, 1970).

Chapter Six: Completing the Coastline

The main source for the travels of Simpson and Dease is Thomas Simpson, *Narrative of Discoveries on the North Coast of America*, 2 vols. (London: Richard Bentley, 1843), though the author is even more self-aggrandizing than most autobiographers. His brother, Alexander, wrote a biography, *Life and Travels of Thomas Simpson, Arctic Discoverer* (London: 1845). Later theories about Simpson's mysterious death were elaborated in John A. Stevenson, "The Unsolved Death of Thomas Simpson, Explorer," *The Beaver*, outfit 266 (June, 1935) and in Douglas Mackay and W. Kaye Lamb, "More Light on Thomas Simpson," *The Beaver*, outfit 269 (Sept., 1938).

John Rae's own account of his expedition is *Narrative of an Expedition to the Shores of the Arctic Sea in 1846 and 1847* (London: 1850). His letters and a good deal of background information are collected in E. E. Rich and A. M. Johnson, eds., *John Rae's Correspondence with the Hudson's Bay Company on Arctic Exploration, 1844-1855* (London: Hudson Bay Record Society, 1953).

Chapter Seven: Lost and Found: The Search for Franklin

Material on the Franklin search is too voluminous to list exhaustively here. The best history of the events is Leslie Neatby, *Search for Franklin* (Edmonton: Hurtig, 1970). A more academic, analytic study is Hugh N. Wallace, *The Navy, The Company and Richard King 1829-60* (Montreal: McGill-Queen's University Press, 1980). Roderic Owen, *The Fate of Franklin* (London: Hutchinson, 1978) gives a flavour of events in Britain during the search. The politics of the search are described in Clive Holland, "The Arctic Committee of 1851," *Polar Record*, 2 parts, vol. 20 (Jan. and May, 1980).

A few of the major documentary sources are: Robert M. McClure, *The Discovery of the North-West Passage* (London: Longman, 1851); L. H. Neatby, ed., *Frozen Ships: The Arctic Diary of Johann Miertsching, 1850-54* (New York: St. Martin's Press, 1967); and F. L. McClintock, *The Voyage of the Fox in the Arctic Seas* (London: John Murray, 1859).

Chapter Eight: Search for the Pole

Hall's first expedition to Frobisher Bay is described in his *Life with the Esquimaux* (London: Sampson Low, 1864. Reprinted Edmonton: Hurtig, 1970). His second expedition is the subject of J. E. Nourse, ed., *Narrative of the Second Arctic Expedition Made By Charles F. Hall, 1864-69* (Washington: Government Printing Bureau, 1879). The drift of the *Polaris* is described from George Tyson's point of view in E. Vale Blake, ed., *Arctic Experiences* (New York: Harper, 1874). An excellent biography of Hall is Chauncey Loomis, *Weird and Tragic Shores: The Story of Charles Francis Hall, Explorer* (New York: Alfred Knopf, 1971).

Other sources for different expeditions up Smith Sound include George W. Corner, *Doctor Kane of the Arctic Seas* (Philadelphia: Temple University Press, 1972), a biography of Elisha Kent Kane; G. Hattersley-Smith, "The British Arctic Expedition, 1875-76," *Polar Record*, vol. 18, no. 113 (1976), an account of the Nares expedition; and C. J. Taylor, "First International Polar Year, 1882-83," *Arctic*, vol. 34, no. 4 (December, 1981), a description of events surrounding the Greeley expedition.

Chapter Nine: The Scandinavians

Otto Sverdrup's own account of his arctic travels is *New Land* (London: Longmans, 1904). An abridged version, with biographical material, is T. C. Fairley, ed., *Sverdrup's Arctic Adventures* (London: Longmans, 1959). The voyage of the *Gjoa* is recounted in Roald Amundsen, *The North West Passage* (New York: E. P. Dutton, 1908). A stimulating, controversial book about Amundsen, and the Norwegian school of exploration generally, is Roland Huntford, *Scott and Amundsen* (London: Hodder & Stoughton, 1979).

Chapter Ten: Canada Claims the Arctic

Vilhjalmur Stefansson wrote several books about his arctic experiences, including *My Life with the Eskimo* (New York: Macmillan, 1913); *The Friendly Arctic* (New York: Macmillan, 1921); and *Hunters of the Great North* (New York: Harcourt, Brace, 1922). An excellent study of Stefansson's experience with the Canadian Arctic Expedition is Richard J. Diubaldo, *Stefansson and the Canadian Arctic* (Montreal: McGill-Queen's University Press, 1978).

The earlier expeditions are described in A. P. Low, *The Cruise of the Neptune, 1903-04* (Ottawa: Government Printing

Bureau, 1906) and the relevant annual reports of the federal Department of Marine and Fisheries. Captain Bernier's role is discussed in Yolande Dorion-Robitaille, *Captain J. E. Bernier's Contribution to Canadian Sovereignty in the Arctic* (Ottawa: Indian & Northern Affairs, 1978).

Three interesting studies of different stages of the sovereignty issue are: G. W. Smith, "The Transfer of Arctic Territories from Great Britain to Canada in 1880, and some Related Matters, as seen in Official Correspondence," *Arctic*, vol. 14, no. 1 (March, 1961); W. Gillies Ross, "Canadian Sovereignty in the Arctic: The Neptune Expedition of 1903–04," *Arctic*, vol. 29, no. 2 (June, 1976); D. W. Dinwoodie, "Arctic Controversy: The 1925 Byrd-MacMillan Expedition Example," *Canadian Historical Review*, vol. LIII, no. 1 (March, 1972).

Arctic whaling activities are described in three books: Daniel Francis, *Arctic Chase: A History of Whaling in Canada's North* (St. John's: Breakwater, 1984); John Bockstoce, *Steam Whaling in the Western Arctic* (New Bedford, Mass.: Old Dartmouth Historical Society, 1977); and W. Gillies Ross, *Whaling and Eskimos: Hudson Bay, 1860–1915* (Ottawa: National Museum of Man, 1975). A general overview of northern history during the period is Morris Zaslow, *The Opening of the Canadian North, 1870–1914* (Toronto: McClelland & Stewart, 1971).

Index